The VW Air-Cooled Engine

Repair and Maintenance

The VW Air-Cooled Engine

Repair and Maintenance

Ken Cservenka

THE CROWOOD PRESS

First published in 2018 by
The Crowood Press Ltd
Ramsbury, Marlborough
Wiltshire SN8 2HR

www.crowood.com

© Ken Cservenka 2018

All rights reserved. No part of this publication may be reproduced or transmitted in any form or by any means, electronic or mechanical, including photocopy, recording, or any information storage and retrieval system, without permission in writing from the publishers.

British Library Cataloguing-in-Publication Data
A catalogue record for this book is available from the British Library.

ISBN 978 1 78500 375 2

Typeset by Jean Cussons Typesetting, Diss, Norfolk

Printed and bound in India by Replika Press Pvt. Ltd.

CONTENTS

Preface and Acknowledgements   6

1.	Workshop Essentials	7
2.	The Type 1 Engine: Keeping it Healthy	12
3.	Engine Removal	30
4.	Removing the Exhaust and Ancillaries on Type 1 Engines	42
5.	Engine Strip-Down	51
6.	Examination of the Engine Components	68
7.	Assembling the Crankshaft	71
8.	Rebuilding the Crankcase	78
9.	Removing the Exhaust and Ancillaries on 1700, 1800 and 2-Litre Type 4 Engines	91
10.	Reassembling the Pistons and Cylinders	98
11.	Rebuilding and Installing the Cylinder Heads	100
12.	Replacing Ancillaries and Exhaust on Type 1 Engines	104
13.	Replacing Ancillaries on 1700, 1800 and 2-Litre Type 4 Engines	115

Appendix I: Specifications   123
Appendix II: Engine and Chassis Numbers   135
Useful Addresses   136
Glossary   139
Index   141

PREFACE

I was first introduced to the Volkswagen marque by a family friend of one of my school friends; from memory, it was an oval-windowed 1955 model and I was fascinated by the engine note, the fact that it always started within seconds and the glowing reports from the owner. I then thought nothing more about Volkswagens until I visited a friend down in Devon who owned a 1967 1500 Beetle. We went out in the Beetle and on the way to his home I was asked if I wanted to drive it, a chance I jumped at. As we were travelling at 40mph in top gear my friend told me to press the clutch pedal, which I did. My friend then slammed the gear lever into second and told me to release the clutch pedal. The car screamed in protest but my friend stated that in any other car the gearbox would have exploded. I was already hooked before this amazing demonstration and on Guy Fawkes night 1969 I bought my first Beetle – a 1963 1200 Deluxe. I drove that car until 1983 and covered over 160,000 miles, including camping trips with my wife and three children with all the gear. I then bought a 1968 auto stick-shift Beetle; and in 1989 a 1974 Bay Window camper, a Devon Eurovette conversion, joined the fleet. I also own a 1967 1500 Beetle and it is this car that is featured in the Type 1 engine rebuild in this book. I moved to the Cirencester area in 1972 and as well as repairing my own Beetle I repaired and serviced many air-cooled Beetles and Type 2 vehicles from the local area. In writing this book my aim was to produce a no-nonsense engine manual that any practical-minded person can understand, with a step-by-step guide to building a Type 1 engine. Most operations described can be applied to the Type 4 unit used in 1700, 1800 and 2-litre Transporter models as well. I have deliberately not gone into such technicalities as blueprinting as it is unnecessary on an engine built for everyday usage.

ACKNOWLEDGEMENTS

I would like to thank the following for their help in producing this book: Richard Copping for encouraging me to write this book; Neil Birkitt for looking over my words and helpful advice; the guys at the Engine Shop, especially Jim Gray, for the machine work on the crankcase and crankshaft; Richard Hulin for further machine work and for allowing me the run of his workshop to take photographs of a Type 4 engine; and finally my wife, Mary, for her patience and understanding.

CHAPTER 1

WORKSHOP ESSENTIALS

The Volkswagen air-cooled engine is relatively simple to maintain and repair and, although the flat-four layout is fairly unconventional today, a few well-chosen garage essentials and tools are all that is needed for the home mechanic to be able to tackle most jobs.

A good start is the tool kit that was supplied with the car, consisting of a body jack, a few useful spanners, hub cap-removal tool and a double-ended box spanner. One end of the box spanner is for removal of the wheel bolts while the other end doubles as a spark plug removal tool and is the correct size to remove or tighten the nut on the generator – especially useful for replacing a broken fan belt out on the highway.

However, the body jack should only be used to change a wheel in the event of a puncture out on the road, as it isn't suitable for any major repairs. The tool kit supplied with the car should be kept in the car with a few additions for problems encountered when away from home. I personally carry the tools shown in Figs 1.2 and 1.3.

Some of the repair procedures described in this book involve using heat, either a blowlamp or boiling water, so for safety wear leather welding gloves, as the components are very hot to handle. When using a blowlamp or in any situation where metal fragments may become airborne, always protect your eyes with safety glasses or goggles. (Fig 1.1)

Good-quality spanners are a must for a well-equipped workshop, with both ring and open-ended ones having their uses. When buying ring spanners, look for ones where the effort is exerted on the flat of the nut, not the corners. Buy sets that include the range of sizes from 6mm to 22mm. Additional sizes that are useful are 30mm for the crankshaft pulley nut, and 21mm for the generator pulley nut, though the VW box spanner will do for the latter.

Other useful tools to carry in the vehicle or at your workshop include locking pliers, often referred to

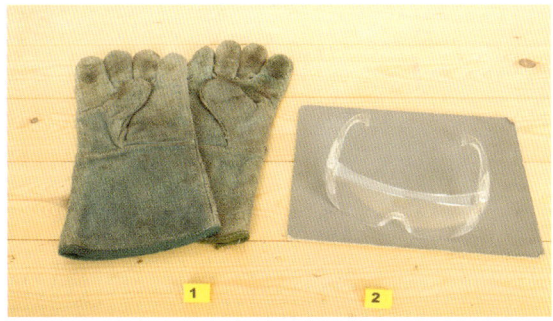

Fig 1.1 Safety equipment includes leather welding gloves for handling hot components and safety glasses.

Fig 1.2 Spanners for maintenance of air-cooled Volkswagen engines: 1) ring spanners, 6–22mm; 2) additional 21mm spanner for generator pulley nut, Type 1 engine; 3) open-ended spanners, 6–22mm; 4) additional 30mm combination spanner for the crankshaft pulley nut, Type 1 engine.

8 WORKSHOP ESSENTIALS

by the trade names of mole grips or vice grips. The expandable pliers (gas pliers) used by the plumbing trade are another valuable addition, as are regular pliers. Feeler gauges and various sizes of screwdriver are used for valve clearances and adjusting the contact breaker points or spark plug gaps. Finally, no toolbox should be without a hammer – though not to be used on the crankcase or cylinder heads.

For more advanced work the following tools have specific roles when rebuilding an air-cooled Volkswagen engine. Allen key bolts and those with a 12pt internal spline are used mostly on the 1700, 1800 and 2-litre engines. When rebuilding the crankshaft on earlier Type 1 engines, a centre punch is used to peen the rim of the nut into an indentation on the connecting rod. When measuring the crankshaft end float using feeler gauges, a micrometer is used to select the third shim. The flywheel oil seal on Type 1 engines is pressed in using a circular tool in conjunction with the flywheel retaining bolt. This can also be achieved with a block of wood and a mallet. When installing the cylinder barrel over the piston it is advisable to use a piston ring clamp as the rings are easily broken.

When stripping down or assembling the gears onto the crankshaft, they are held in place by a circlip. However, the usual style of circlip pliers with pointed ends to grip the holes in the circlip are useless for this job; instead, use circlip pliers with stout flattened jaws that insert between the ends of the circlip to open it out.

When removing the valves from the cylinder head, an extendable magnet or long-nosed pliers are essential to retrieve the collets.

The petrol tank on first- and second-generation Transporter models is situated above the engine; it is therefore essential to clamp the flexible pipe before disconnecting it from the engine. The pipe should be plugged and the clamp removed to avoid damaging the rubber pipe.

It often becomes apparent when working on an

Fig 1.3 Other basic tools for working on the air-cooled engines: 1) locking pliers; 2) expanding pliers; 3) pliers; 4) metric feeler gauges; 5) assortment of screwdrivers; 6) hammer.

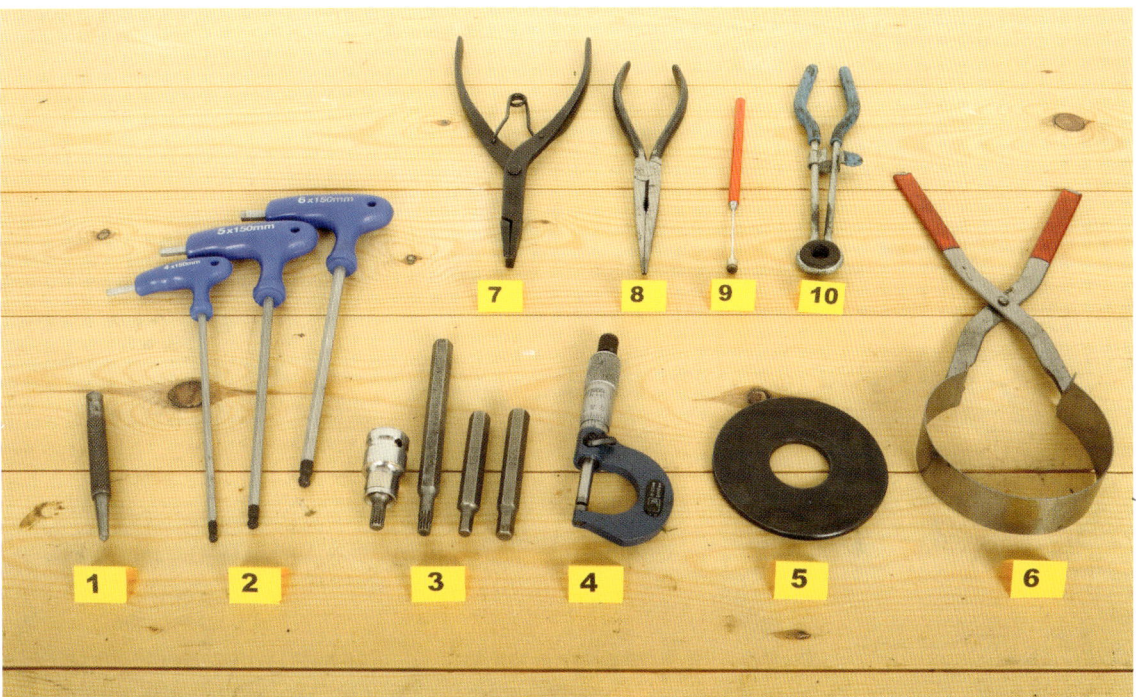

Fig 1.4 Specialist tools for more advanced engine work: 1) centre punch; 2) Allen keys; 3) twelve-point, 8mm socket and Allen key inserts; 4) micrometer; 5) tool to press in crankshaft oil seal; 6) piston-ring clamp; 7) flat-ended circlip pliers; 8) long-nosed pliers; 9) extendable magnet; 10) pipe clamp.

engine that special tools used by the dealer are not readily available, so it becomes necessary to apply a bit of ingenuity to either make or adapt tools to complete the job. For example Fig 1.5 shows a puller made specially to remove a particularly stubborn crankshaft pulley. The rubber suction valve-grinding tool illustrated is readily available from most motor factors or tool suppliers. A length of stout wire from a coat hanger has its uses, such as installing the thrust washers at the base of the distributor drive shaft and positioning the anti-chatter spring in the depression in the top of the shaft. When installing the cylinder barrels over the pistons, lengths of copper tube in conjunction with a cylinder head washer and nut hold the barrel in place while the crankshaft is turned to present the next piston.

A wooden peg, whittled to fit the depression in the distributor drive shaft, is used when removing or installing the shaft. If it proves to be stubborn to remove, an expensive tool is available but in this situation it is better to remove the shaft when the crankcase is opened.

When removing a piston, a Beetle king pin or similar is useful for drifting the pin out. The wire clips in Fig 1.5 were packing pieces used to hold a piece of machinery and were about to be thrown out. They have proved to be very useful for holding the cam followers in the right-hand case half when assembling an engine.

When installing the cam gear, spacer and distributor drive gear onto the crankshaft, always wear leather welding gloves as they are very hot when removed from the boiling water. A length of metal tubing from a local metal supplier is a useful home-made tool to drift the gears into position. Flat-ended circlip pliers are used to install the circlip.

A well-equipped workshop will have the necessary tools to remove and install the clutch. The best option to hold the clutch-driven plate in position is a gearbox input shaft obtained from a scrap

10 WORKSHOP ESSENTIALS

Fig 1.5   Home-made or adapted tools also have a role in advanced engine work. With the exception of item 2, all the items shown here are home-made or adapted from other uses: 1) home-made puller for removing the crankshaft pulley on Type 1 engines; 2) rubber suction tool for valve grinding; 3) a length of stout wire made from a coat hanger used to install the two washers in the distributor driveshaft bore and the anti-chatter spring in the top of the shaft; 4) copper tubes used to retain the cylinder barrels; 5) wooden tool for removing and installing the distributor driveshaft; 6) a Beetle king pin, now a drift for installing piston pins; 7) wire spring clips to retain cam followers.

Fig 1.6   Installing the two gears and the spacer onto the crankshaft: 1) a length of steel tubing purchased from a local metal supplier makes a suitable drift; 2) the flat-ended circlip pliers are used to fit the retaining circlip; 3) a gunmetal hammer will not damage steel components.

Fig 1.7   1) Gearbox input shaft used to hold the drive plate when installing the clutch pressure plate; 2) a plastic tool for holding the clutch plate; 3) flywheel lock; 4) a length of angle iron bolted to the flywheel using the clutch bolts is a safer option for holding the flywheel when tightening the high-torque bolt used on the Type 1 engine ; 5) torque wrench and 13mm socket for tightening the clutch bolts.

Fig 1.8 1) a ½in-drive socket set; 2) a ⅜in-drive long-reach and short socket sets and ratchet driver; 3) a 1in-drive 36mm socket and sliding T-bar for tightening the flywheel-retaining bolt; 4) torque wrench with a range of 5–40lb ft (7–54Nm).

gearbox. Plastic tools to replicate the input shaft are also available. When fitting the clutch, use a flywheel locking tool that bolts to the top nut on the crankcase. It is best to lock the flywheel in position using a length of angle iron bolted between two of the clutch bolt holes.

A socket set is always a good investment; ½in drive socket sets were the preferred choice when I obtained mine in the late 1960s, but ⅜ drive sets are now widely available and are often the preferred choice, especially when there is limited access. A ¾ or 1in drive 36mm socket and sliding T bar is necessary to remove and install the high torque flywheel bolt on Type 1 engines. Another essential when working on engines is a torque wrench with a range of 5lb ft (7Nm) to 40lb ft (54Nm).

A trolley jack with a good maximum lift height and axle stands are essential for removing or installing the air-cooled engines. Unlike other makes, which remove the engine with a crane through the bonnet aperture, the Volkswagen air-cooled engine is removed from under the vehicle. A pair of solid wooden blocks is useful for lowering the engine onto before removing any blocks used between the engine and the jack.

Fig 1.9 A trolley jack and axle stands are essential when removing or installing the air-cooled engine. The blocks are a useful addition to stand the unit on.

CHAPTER 2

THE TYPE 1 ENGINE: KEEPING IT HEALTHY

To keep your Volkswagen engine running sweetly and in tip-top condition, there are maintenance procedures that need relatively frequent attention. Unlike vehicles produced in the twenty-first century, we don't have the luxury of service intervals of 10,000 miles or more. Instead, the Type 1 engine requires checking weekly, with the major service scheduled for every 3,000 miles or 5,000km.

To illustrate this point, a good example is the fan belt, which not only drives the large fan that provides the all-important cooling air to the cylinders and cylinder heads, but also drives the generator to keep the battery topped up. A slack belt will prevent the fan from supplying sufficient cooling air at higher speeds and will also starve the battery of the power to keep it at maximum efficiency.

WEEKLY CHECKS, EVERY 300 MILES OR 500KM

1. Fan belt tension; check 300 miles after fitting a new belt (see 3,000-mile service below).
2. Engine oil level.

ENGINE SERVICE, EVERY 3,000 MILES OR 5,000KM

1. Check and adjust fan belt tension.
2. Change engine oil and clean oil strainer.
3. Clean and service air filter.
4. Clean fuel pump filter (early engines only).
5. Check the condition of ignition leads, distributor cap and rotor arm.
6. Clean and adjust contact breaker points.
7. Check and reset ignition timing.
8. Check spark plugs.
9. Check clutch pedal free play.
10. Check valve clearances (adjust tappets).

FAN BELT TENSION, TYPE 1 ENGINE

As this is an air-cooled engine, a spare fan belt and the necessary tools to replace it should always be kept in the vehicle. If the belt breaks, indicated by the red ignition warning light coming on, stop the vehicle as soon as it is safe to do so and switch the engine off. While the car can continue for some time before the battery goes flat, the Type 1 engine will quickly overheat and be rendered irreparable without the cooling effect of the fan.

Generally, if you can see the fan belt flexing when the engine is running, it will need adjusting. To check it properly, first turn off the ignition and remove the key from the switch. Depress the belt halfway between the pulleys; the deflection should be no more than 13mm on the early engines produced before the 1967 model year, or 10mm on the 1500cc engine and all models produced since. If the deflection is more than the above values the belt will need adjusting. Also examine the belt for signs of ageing, cracking or polishing and replace it if in any doubt.

Volkswagen didn't follow the usual route of providing an adjustable belt-tensioning device for the Type

THE TYPE 1 ENGINE: KEEPING IT HEALTHY

Fig 2.1 The fan belt should be free of cracks or fraying. It is wise to keep a spare in the car.

1 engine; instead they used a tapered split generator pulley, fitted with shims between each half. By removing shims the V-shaped fan belt rides higher up the pulley, effectively increasing its diameter to take up any free play.

Fan Belt Adjustment or Replacement (Figs 2.2–2.3)

Tools required:
- Medium to large flat-blade screwdriver
- 21mm ring spanner, socket or the multi-purpose box spanner supplied with the vehicle
- 30mm open-ended or ring spanner (optional)

1. Using the 21mm ring or the multi-purpose box spanner, turn the nut holding the generator pulley clockwise until the cutout on the forward edge of the inner pulley half is just past top centre. Insert the screwdriver so that the tip rests against the top generator housing bolt, thus preventing the pulley from turning while the nut is loosened.
2. Remove the nut, followed by the conical spacer, spare shims and the outer pulley half. There should now be some shims left between the two pulleys; if not, the belt will need replacing. Remove one shim and add it to the pack of spare shims removed before the outer pulley.
3. Before reassembly examine the belt for excessive wear or fraying. If in doubt, replace the belt – your engine's life depends on it! If replacing the belt on later engines, remove the cover over the crankshaft pulley bolt, which is held by three 6mm slotted tinware screws.
4. Fit the belt into the groove of the lower pulley and then offer the belt up to the inner half of the generator pulley. Having already removed a shim from between the pulley halves, fit the outer pulley, taking care to locate the lugs on the outer half into the slots on the inner half. Replace the outer shim pack, including the shim removed from between the pulley halves, followed by the conical spacer and finally the nut. It is easier to allow the engine to rotate while tightening the bolt, as this helps to locate the belt into the correct position. Finally, tighten the nut fully,

Fig 2.2 A screwdriver held against the screw through the cutout in the pulley is used to stop the pulley turning while the nut is undone.

Fig 2.3 The fan belt is adjusted by adding or removing shims between the pulley halves. The spare shims are kept between the domed cap and the pulley.

Fig 2.4   Later models are fitted with a guard over the crankshaft pulley nut. Very early split-window models had a bracket that could be swivelled into position so a starting handle could engage with a dog on the pulley nut.

Part Numbers
111 903 137   Fan belt, width 13mm, 25 PS
111 903 137D   Fan belt, width 9.5mm, all models, dynamo
111 903 137E   Fan belt, width 11.3mm, all models, alternator

GENERATOR BELT ADJUSTMENT OR REPLACEMENT, TYPE 3 ENGINE (FIGS 2.5–2.6)

The engine fitted to the Volkswagen Type 3 is essentially the same unit as fitted to the Type 1. However, the cooling fan is fitted directly to the crankshaft, within an entirely different and flatter housing, giving rise to the unit being described as a 'suitcase-style' engine. The generator is located to the left of the distributor on this engine and the adjustment of its drive belt can be carried out after removal of the air intake housing cover.

having wedged the screwdriver into the slot on the back of the inner pulley but this time against the left-hand edge of the generator housing bolt. Re-check the belt tension and if not satisfied repeat the above procedure. Do not over-tighten the belt, as the extra load can damage the bearings in the generator.

The adjustment procedure is essentially the same as described above for the Type 1, except that the pulley is retained by two nuts. The inner 27mm nut can be held with one spanner while a second spanner loosens the outer 21mm nut.

Fig 2.5   The fan belt adjustment on Type 3 models hides under the black cover to the right of the blue coil.

Fig 2.6 The cover removed on a Type 3 engine to reveal a similar set-up for adjusting the fan belt as found on Type 1 units.

The belt tension is correct when the deflection is 15mm when pressed halfway between the pulleys. From August 1971 this deflection was reduced to 6mm.

ENGINE OIL LEVEL (FIG 2.7)

The engine oil is an important component of the cooling system, along with the airflow created by the fan. The oil serves as a heat sink, and is cooled by the airflow from the fan as it passes through the oil cooler mounted within the fan housing. Insufficient oil volume can cause the engine to run hot.

It is just as important not to overfill the engine, as the pulley end of the crankshaft doesn't have an oil seal; instead, the crankshaft is fitted with a concave oil deflector plate to steer any stray oil back into the crankcase. This plate is ineffective if the engine is overfilled, resulting in oil leaking out behind the pulley and being sprayed all over the engine compartment.

The oil level should be checked weekly, or before any long journey is undertaken, and topped up to no higher than the top mark on the dipstick. However, never let the level fall below the lower mark. It takes half a litre of oil to fill between the top and lower marks on the dipstick.

Fig 2.7 Oil filler cap and dipstick as fitted on all Type 1 engines.

Engine Oil Change and Oil Strainer Clean (Figs 2.8–2.10)

Tools and parts required:
- 21mm ring spanner, socket or the multi-purpose box spanner supplied with the vehicle
- 10mm ring spanner or socket
- Oil drain pan (DIY tip: use a 5-litre plastic container with a hole cut in the flat side)
- Container for the used oil
- Disposable gloves
- Oil-change gasket set
- Oil filter (from August 1992 only, Mexican-built Beetle models)
- Suitable oil filter removal tool for late Mexican Beetle models
- Oil
- Funnel

16 THE TYPE 1 ENGINE: KEEPING IT HEALTHY

Oil capacity:
- 2.5 litres for all models except Mexican-built models with fuel injection
- 3 litres for Mexican cars with fuel injection, and for T3 CT engine

Torque wrench settings:
- 6mm cap nuts   10mm socket   5lb ft (7Nm)
- Drain plug   21mm socket   25lb ft (34Nm)

1. Run the engine up to operating temperature, as the oil drains more efficiently when warm. The oil change can be performed without raising the car on saloon models running at factory-set ride height, but access is easier if the rear of the vehicle is raised a little. Always use axle stands when working beneath the vehicle.
2. With the oil drain pan in place and your hands protected from the detrimental effects of dirty oil, release and remove the drain plug, if fitted, from the centre-mounted oil strainer cover, using the 21mm spanner. It's worth noting here that later models were fitted with a strainer plate cover without a centrally mounted drain plug. However, most owners soon opted to fit the earlier cover, as it's a messy business draining the oil without a drain plug.

   For this reason, on later models don't remove the cover completely until all the oil has drained or you will have more oil up your arm than in the drain pan. The technique with these later engines is to loosen all the nuts before removing five completely. Leave the last nut loose but not removed, and detach the strainer plate cover on one side using a screwdriver. Before draining the oil, it helps to undo the oil filler cap.
3. When all the oil has drained from the engine, remove the cover plate, strainer plate and gaskets. Clean the oil strainer gauze and cover plate using engine cleaner or petrol, being careful to remove any traces of sludge or grit.
4. Remove all traces of gasket material from the mating surfaces and reassemble using new gaskets from the oil-change kit and new copper washers on the 6mm studs. Take extreme care

Fig 2.8 Cover under the engine for the oil strainer. Some later engines didn't have a drain plug.

Fig 2.9 The drain plug is removed with a 21mm socket or spanner.

Fig 2.10 Take care not to strip the thread on the oil strainer cap nuts. The thread is 6mm so only torque to 5lb ft (7Nm).

when tightening the six cap nuts as the studs are easy to break. Use a short 10mm spanner or a torque wrench set to 5lb ft (7Nm) to avoid exerting too much pressure. Use a new copper compression ring on the drain plug before refitting and tightening to the required torque, 25lb ft (34Nm).

Fitting of a magnetic drain plug is recommended to catch and trap any ferrous metal particles that find their way into the crankcase.

5. For the Mexican Beetle from August 1992 on and the CT series engine used in 1979–82 T3 Transporters only: using a suitable removal tool, unscrew the spin-on oil filter canister. Rub a smear of oil on the sealing ring of the new filter and tighten firmly, by hand only.
6. Finally, refill the engine with good quality oil. This is not as easy as it sounds, due to the angle of the filler neck. To avoid spillage, use a funnel.

At the time of manufacture, Volkswagen recommended the use solely of a monograde SAE 30 HD oil (SAE being the Society of Automotive Engineers), formulated for use in gasoline engines. This was because multigrade oils were unreliable at the time. Due to the detergent qualities of HD oil, it becomes black and dirty-looking soon after an oil change. However, it is uneconomical and unnecessary to change the oil before the recommended service interval. SAE 30 oil is suitable for use in a temperate climate, as in the UK. In colder climates SAE 20 should be used if the ambient temperature dips to around −15°C. If the ambient temperature is predominately lower than −15°C, use SAE 10. Since 1975, due to the advances in oil technology, Volkswagen has recommended the use of multigrade oil that conforms to the API (American Petroleum Institute) standard, such as SAE 15W-40. This operates efficiently at a much wider temperature range, maintaining a protective layer between the moving parts.

The subject of oil has caused much controversy between owners of air-cooled Volkswagens, with those of the old school doggedly sticking to monograde oil, often preferring the use of an oil formulated for diesel engines, while others have embraced the new technology of modern multigrade; the choice is yours.

Always dispose of oil responsibly; it's illegal to tip it down a drain. Councils always have an oil disposal unit at their recycling centres, and some garages run their heating unit on used oil, so it's always worth asking at your local car repair centre.

CLEANING AND SERVICING THE AIR FILTER (FIGS 2.11–2.17)

The 1131cc, 25 PS engine was fitted with several designs of air cleaner, with a mushroom-shaped filter superseded by a cylindrical filter (known in enthusiast circles as the coffee-can filter) being the most common types. All have one thing in common: they can't be dismantled for cleaning.

To service, remove the air filter from the carburettor and, while observing the necessary precautions when using volatile liquids, pour petrol or other cleaning fluid into the tube that connects the filter body to the carburettor until the liquid runs clear through the air intake holes. Allow the filter to dry before reassembly.

From the last week of 1953 until the early days of the 1973 model year an oil bath air filter was used. In the Beetle this sat directly on top of the carburettor, while for other models, including the Karmann Ghia, Transporter and military-derived vehicles such as the Type 181, the fitment was described as suspended, as the filter itself sat remotely on a bracket with a length of rubber tubing connecting it to the carburettor. As the years progressed, the arrangements became ever more complicated, with cardboard tubing to supply heated air during the warm-up period, a pipe to recycle the crankcase fumes and combined vacuum and thermostatic valves in the intake air preheating system that allowed precise control, depending on both temperature and engine load. The ongoing modifications were added to the specification to satisfy ever more stringent emissions regulations.

LEFT: Fig 2.11 Mushroom air filter fitted to 25PS engines; 26 VFIS carburettor.

BELOW: Fig 2.12 Coffee-can air filter also fitted to 25PS engines.

THE TYPE 1 ENGINE: KEEPING IT HEALTHY

ABOVE: Fig 2.13 Oil bath air filter fitted to the 28 PCI carburettor on 30PS engines.

RIGHT: Fig 2.14 Oil bath air-cleaner as used in the mid-1960s. The carburettor is a 30 PICT-1 or 30 PICT-2 on a 1300 F-series engine.

Fig 2.15 Oil bath air cleaner as used on a 1500 H-series engine. The carburettor is a 30 PICT-1 or 30 PICT-2 jetted to suit the larger-capacity engine.

However, the service requirements are the same for all oil bath filters and in most cases can be undertaken without removing the complete unit. Unclip the top half, having removed and marked for reinstallation any hoses connected to it. Carefully lift the top section clear of the bowl, without tipping, and set it down on a clean surface. Do not turn the top half over as any dirty oil present will enter and contaminate the top section of the unit. Check that the oil level in the bowl is up to the mark and there isn't an excessive build-up of sludge. It's usually only necessary to change the oil every second service unless the vehicle has been used in exceptionally dusty conditions.

To clean the lower section, the unit will need to be removed from the vehicle, having unclipped any hoses, breather pipes and in some cases a bowden cable connected to the thermostat. Mark any vacuum hoses removed as it's absolutely vital that they are not muddled. If the hoses are replaced incorrectly, the manifold vacuum can collapse the fuel tank on Type 2 models.

On models where the lower housing is fitted directly to the carburettor, undo the clamping screw; or for models using a remote filter, release the clips holding the lower section in place.

Type 2 models from 1963 on have an oil filter mounted on a bracket to the right of the engine compartment, held in place by clips. On these models it's easier to disconnect the connecting hose from the carburettor and remove the complete remote filter. Clean the lower bowl of the filter using petrol or solvent such as brake cleaner. Generally, the upper section can be fitted after simply wiping around the lower flange that sits in the oil.

However, if the filter has been neglected, the holes into the top section may be blocked and need scraping to remove any sludge build-up. To clean the top section, stand it in a suitable container partly filled with a solvent such as paraffin. To eliminate the risk of the solvent contaminating the oil in the filter bowl, blow dry the element if possible using an airline, before allowing the top section to dry thoroughly prior to refitting. Fit the lower section and connect all the hoses and cables in the correct order before filling with oil up to the mark. Refit the top section and reconnect any hoses removed earlier. Again, with Type 2 models from 1963 on, it's easier to refill with oil and fit the two halves together before attaching the complete unit to the bracket.

Some owners, especially those who have fitted an aftermarket carburettor set-up, will also have suitable, but non-standard, air filter units fitted, such as K&N. Some types, such as K&N aftermarket filter elements, are reusable after cleaning and oiling, while others have a paper filter, which should be

Fig 2.16 The downward-pointing arrow in this oil bath filter bowl indicated the maximum oil level. Sometimes a red line was used instead.

replaced during a service. In all cases it's advisable to follow the manufacturer's recommendations.

Beetle and Transporter models were fitted with paper element air filters from early in the 1973 model year, with other models receiving the same modification soon after. The element should be replaced every 18,000 miles, sooner if used in dusty conditions. However, a blast with an airline is sometimes all that is needed to clean the paper element. To replace the paper element on some vehicles, the

Fig 2.17 This late model with a 1600 50PS engine is fitted with a replaceable paper element air filter.

complete filter housing will need to be removed, after marking the position of any hoses or vacuum lines to aid reassembly. It is then a simple matter of releasing several clips to gain access to the filter element. Clean the lower section of the filter housing before fitting the new paper element.

FUEL PUMP

On the 25 and 30PS engines built up to August 1960, the fuel pump was mounted on the left side of the crankcase, driven by a horizontal pushrod acting on an eccentric cam at the base of the distributor driveshaft. The only exception to this was the Transporter engine introduced in May 1959. This unit still only produced 30PS but followed the style of the 34PS engine introduced for all models in August 1959 for the 1960 model year. This redesigned unit has a new style of pump mounted on the top of the crankcase driven by a vertical pushrod, again actuated by an eccentric cam at the base of the distributor driveshaft. Both types of pump are mounted on an intermediate plastic flange that acts as a steady bearing for the pushrod. Pushrod stroke, and hence fuel pressure, can be adjusted by adding an extra gasket, but the minimum of one gasket each side of the intermediate flange must always be fitted.

From March 1972 a fuel pump with a pressed casing was used and this unit cannot be serviced. This prompted many owners to fit an inline fuel filter. This style of pump can often be found on engines produced after 1960 as a replacement for the original equipment. This later pressed casing style of pump is produced in two patterns, with the version produced for vehicles fitted with an alternator tilted at an angle to avoid interference with the larger-diameter alternator casing.

CLEANING THE FUEL PUMP FILTER (EARLY ENGINES ONLY)

For obvious reasons, it's advisable not to work on the fuel system when the engine is hot. Always use metal pipe clips on the braided rubber fuel lines and never replace these with inferior plastic tubing. Always use the correct size of hose and don't over-tighten the hose clamps. All of the above can lead to a barbecued engine or, in the worst cases, the entire vehicle.

25 AND 30PS ENGINES (FIG 2.12)

Tools required:
- 14mm spanner or socket
- Small paint brush
- Fire extinguisher

It is always a good idea to have a fire extinguisher handy and to carry one in the car at all times.

Remove the plug situated on the top of the pump and remove the cone-shaped filter. Using a brush – never a fluffy cloth – wash the filter in white spirit or fuel and thoroughly dry, before refitting it pointed end uppermost. Replace the washer, if damaged, and after refitting the plug run the engine and check for fuel leaks.

34PS AND ALL LATER ENGINES (FIG 2.18)

All pumps fitted after August 1959 are situated on the top of the crankcase and are available in three main types. Those pumps with a single screw or bolt through the top cover are fitted with a filter across the entire diameter of the pump.

Fig 2.18 *This fuel pump has a removable top, which enables the internal filter to be removed for cleaning. It is now common to find pumps that are sealed units.*

THE TYPE 1 ENGINE: KEEPING IT HEALTHY

Those with a hexagonal plug facing the rear of the vehicle have a cone-shaped filter behind the plug. The third type of pump, which was fitted to the later vehicles, is also often found on earlier models as a replacement after the original pump has failed. These are sealed and cannot be dismantled for servicing.

Clamp the flexible fuel hose leading to the pump body from the fuel tank and unscrew the single bolt or screw from the top cover to gain access to the filter. For later models, remove the hexagonal plug facing the rear of the vehicle and remove the cone-shaped filter. Clean as instructed in the previous section and replace in reverse order. The cone-shaped filter is fitted with the pointed end towards the plug.

It's not a bad idea – in fact, it's recommended on those vehicles with a sealed fuel pump – to install an inline fuel filter before the fuel pump. To aid installation, these are usually marked with the direction of fuel flow.

IGNITION LEADS, DISTRIBUTOR CAP AND ROTOR ARM

Ideally, work on the distributor when the engine is cold. This is particularly important when checking the static timing (*see* below).

All dust and dirt should be removed from these components to prevent sparks from tracking to earth, as this could lead to poor starting or a misfire. In the event of poor starting on a damp day it is OK to use a spray such as WD40 to expel the dampness, but clean the leads and distributor cap at the earliest opportunity, as the dust and dirt will stick to the spray as it begins to dry out, making the starting problem worse. Remove the rotor arm and clean off any black deposits on the brass contact. Also clean the inside of the distributor cap and carefully check it for cracks. A cracked distributor cap should be replaced.

CONTACT BREAKER POINTS

With the rotor arm removed, rotate the engine to line up the cam follower with the high point on the cam. With the points open, it's possible to check the condition of the contact breaker surfaces. If there's a raised lump on one contact surface and a corresponding dent in the other, it will be impossible to set the correct gap and they will need to be removed to clean them up, or replaced.

The one-piece points assembly is attached to the top plate of the distributor by a single screw on most late models, while earlier vehicles have a two-piece contact point assembly with additional screws and insulating washers holding the moving contact. On these earlier vehicles care must be taken to observe the correct order of the parts during removal to aid reassembly later.

Minor pitting of the surface of the points can be cleaned up using a small file. Excessive pitting may indicate that the condenser is due for replacement, and in this case the points should be replaced also. When refitting the points, tighten the screw on the fixed contact just enough to allow the plate to be moved. There are two raised dots on the top plate of the distributor and a cutout portion on the end of the fixed contact. The raised dots are provided to anchor one side of the screwdriver blade while the other side fits into the cutout on the fixed contact, thus allowing fine adjustment of the contact points. The feeler gauge should be a drag fit between the points, 0.40mm or 0.016in. When satisfied with the adjustment, tighten the screw while holding the fixed contact plate in position with another screwdriver.

STATIC IGNITION TIMING (FIG 2.19)

It's important to realize that Volkswagen fitted a multitude of different distributors over the production run of the Type 1 engine, many with different advance curves, necessitating the use of different timing marks. Most were 7.5° before top dead centre (BTDC), while some early models – 1960 to August 1965 – were 10° BTDC. Some later engines were fitted with distributors timed at TDC and even 5° ATDC. However, these were mostly used to satisfy ever more stringent USA emissions regulations.

This all went out of the window when owners fitted either a different distributor from another engine or replaced the original worn-out distributor with an all-centrifugal advance unit such as the Bosch 009, timed at 7.5° BTDC. To recap, the distributor type decides which timing mark should be used.

Some owners have fitted aftermarket aluminium crankshaft pulleys with all the degrees marked on a band around the rim. These make it easier to check the total advance at higher revolutions using a strobe timing light. Total advance at higher revolutions shouldn't exceed 28° BTDC.

All original Volkswagen pulleys have a depression on the face indicating TDC; a single notch to the right indicates 7.5° BTDC, while the two notches to the right of TDC are 7.5° BTDC for the left notch and 10° BTDC for the right-hand indentation. A notch to the left of the TDC depression indicates 5° ATDC.

Tools required:
- 10mm ⅜in drive socket or ring spanner
- Timing light (bulb holder and lead)
- 30mm ring spanner

Static ignition timing must be carried out with the engine stone cold, preferably after being left overnight.

1. With the distributor cap removed, rotate the engine using the 30mm ring spanner on the crankshaft pulley nut until the rotor arm points towards the notch on the rim of the distributor, indicating no. 1 cylinder, and the appropriate v-shaped static timing mark to the right of the top dead centre mark on the crankshaft pulley lines up with the joint between the two crankcase halves. The v-shaped mark on the crankshaft pulley also indicates the timing mark for no. 3 cylinder, so it's important to check the rotor arm is pointing towards the groove on the rim of the distributor body to avoid any ambiguity.
2. Connect a timing light to terminal 1 on the coil. The timing light can be as simple as a bulb in a holder with a length of wire and a female spade

Fig 2.19 With no. 1 cylinder at TDC, the rotor arm should be pointing at the notch in the rim of the distributor body.

connector. Earth the bulb holder or earth wire from the timing light to the crankcase.
3. Release the clamp at the base of the distributor just enough to allow the body to turn (using a 10mm spanner).
4. Switch on the ignition and rotate the body of the distributor clockwise a little way, or until the timing light comes on at the next peak of the cam. This will allow for any slack in the components. Then, very slowly, turn the distributor anticlockwise until the timing light comes on for number 1 cylinder and then tighten the distributor clamp. If you were careful when rotating the engine anti-clockwise the timing should now be set.
5. Rotate the engine clockwise one compete cycle to check that the timing light comes on exactly when the timing mark for no. 1 cylinder lines up with the crankcase joint. If not, repeat actions 3 and 4.

Many owners have fitted an aftermarket electronic ignition system (such as the Pertronix) to simplify maintenance and, in most cases, improve performance and starting.

SPARK PLUGS (FIGS 2.20–2.21)

Tools required:
- Multi-purpose box spanner that was supplied with the vehicle, or standard-size spark plug socket and ratchet wrench

THE TYPE 1 ENGINE: KEEPING IT HEALTHY

- Universal or flexible joint for the socket wrench
- Set of feeler gauges
- Small brass wire brush

1. Warm up the engine, but not too much, before removing the spark plugs. This helps to loosen the plugs without stripping the thread. If you do strip the spark plug thread, you will need to remove the engine to take off the cylinder head and have a helicoil insert fitted by a competent engine repair specialist!
2. With the plugs removed, clean off any carbon deposits using the brass brush before checking the electrode gap. Replace the plugs if the electrodes are showing excessive wear. Set the gaps to 0.7mm (0.028in).

   Tip for daily drivers: set the gaps to 0.6mm (0.025in) in the autumn and you won't need to remove them again until the spring.
3. Check the condition of the rubber sealing rings around the plug caps and replace if split. Take care to ensure that the sealing rings are snug against the cylinder shroud; this is important to prevent the loss of valuable cooling air.
4. Check the condition of the spark plug leads. With the engine running, it's a good idea to look at these when it's dark, to see if you can detect any signs of sparks tracking to earth. If in doubt replace the ignition leads. Also look for signs of tracking at the coil and distributor cap.
5. Finally, check that the plug caps are securely screwed into the ignition leads.

CLUTCH PEDAL FREE PLAY (FIGS 2.22–2.24)

Tools required:
- 10mm ring spanner
- 14mm open-ended spanner
- Mole grips or similar
- Axle stands or ramps

Although not strictly an engine repair operation, this is a procedure you neglect at your peril, as a replacement clutch assembly necessitates the removal of the engine.

Fig 2.20 The spark plug gap should be set to 0.70mm or 0.028in.

Fig 2.21 The sealing ring around the spark plug should be a snug fit against the cylinder shroud.

Fig 2.22 Free play measured at the clutch pedal should be between 10 and 20mm.

THE TYPE 1 ENGINE: KEEPING IT HEALTHY

Measured at the clutch pedal, the free play movement when the pedal is depressed should be between 10 and 20mm before firmer resistance is felt. Less than 10mm and the clutch friction material will wear, while more than 20mm of play will result in the gears crunching during a shift.

The adjustment of the cable is by the lever on the left-hand side of the gearbox, which can be very difficult to reach. Adjustment is best carried out with the vehicle on a garage ramp but can also be done with the car raised on axle stands or drive-on portable ramps.

Before April 1965 the cable was secured by a large nut with a smaller locking nut to hold it in place. The early type can be identified by the curved clutch-operating lever.

After April 1965, a new straight clutch-operating lever was introduced, and this is adjusted by turning a large wing nut in half-turn increments. The shape of the mating surfaces between the nut and the corresponding depression in the clutch operating lever is oblong, which allows the wing nut to click into place every half turn.

Before attempting to adjust the clutch free play, inspect the cable near to the adjusting mechanism for signs of fraying.

Fig 2.23 *With the car body removed, the clutch adjustment arrangement for pre-April 1965 cars can be clearly seen, featuring a large adjustment nut with a smaller lock nut.*

Fig 2.24 *The clutch pedal free play on later cars is simple to adjust. The wing nut clicks into place every half turn, removing the need for a lock nut. However, the wing nut can be stiff to turn unless ample lubricant is applied.*

1. With the vehicle safely raised on a ramp or axle stands, clamp a pair of mole grips onto the cable adjuster rod forward of the clutch-operating lever to prevent the cable from turning.
2. On pre-1965 vehicles, release the lock nut (10mm spanner) and turn the larger nut (14mm) to adjust the free play. To achieve more free play, the adjusting nut should be turned anticlockwise, while less play requires the nut to be tightened clockwise.
3. On post-1965 vehicles simply turn the wing nut in the appropriate direction half a turn at a time. The mating surface of the wing nut readily clicks into place, thus locking it and preventing it from turning. There is a tool available that fits over the wing nut to make it easier to turn.
4. When satisfied with the adjustment, around 13mm or ½in at the pedal, lock the smaller nut tight against the larger adjusting nut on the early vehicles.
5. Finally, remove the mole grips from the cable adjuster and lower the vehicle to the ground.

VALVE CLEARANCES (TAPPET ADJUSTMENT, FIGS 2.25–2.29)

Valve clearances that are too loose will be noisy (tappety) and will rob the engine of power, but if they are too tight they can cause the valve and the valve seat to burn, necessitating their replacement. However, a slightly loose tappet is preferable to one that is too tight.

Tools required:
- Large flat-bladed screwdriver
- Medium flat-bladed screwdriver
- 13mm ring spanner (top tip: use a ½in AF spanner for a really snug fit. There's nothing worse than a spanner that slips)
- Feeler gauges
- 30mm ring spanner

Specifications:
- 30PS engines: 0.10mm (0.004in) for both inlet and exhaust. However, set to 0.15mm(0.006) – see below.
- 34PS engines to December 1963: 0.20mm (0.008in) inlet and 0.30mm (0.012in) exhaust. However, a good proportion of these engines may have been replaced and the clearances changed to the later specification of 0.15mm (0.006in).
- 34PS engines from December 1963 and all subsequent engines: 0.10mm (0.004in) for both inlet and exhaust. From August 1970, after the introduction of the twin-port 1300 and 1302 Super Beetle, Volkswagen increased the valve clearances to 0.15mm (0.006in). This quickly became the norm for all engines previously using the 0.10mm clearances.

It is just about possible to adjust the valve clearances with the car on the ground, but it's more comfortable if the vehicle is raised.

1. Raise the vehicle off the ground and safely support it on axle stands or portable ramps.
2. Using the large screwdriver, lever the spring clamps holding the rocker covers downwards and remove the covers. A small quantity of oil may drain onto the floor from the valve chamber.
3. Check the tightness of the rocker shaft-securing nuts: 18lb ft (25Nm).
4. With the distributor cap removed, rotate the engine using the 30mm spanner on the crankshaft pulley nut until the rotor arm points at the groove in the rim of the distributor body and the TDC indentation on the pulley lines up with the join in the crankcase.

Fig 2.25 Use a screwdriver to pry open the clip that holds the rocker box cover. Pull the clip downwards.

Fig 2.26 Rotate the engine to find TDC on no. 1 cylinder. Check that the rotor arm is pointing at the notch in the rim of the distributor.

THE TYPE 1 ENGINE: KEEPING IT HEALTHY

5. Both valves on no. 1 cylinder (front right) can now be adjusted. Slide the appropriate feeler gauge between the stem of the valve and the tip of the valve adjusting screw.
6. If the tappet needs adjusting, release the 13mm locking nut on the adjusting screw and turn the screw to achieve a drag fit on the feeler blade between the tip of the screw and the valve. When satisfied, hold the screw with the screwdriver and tighten the locking nut. Recheck the adjustment with the feeler gauge and move onto the next valve
7. When satisfied with the clearances on no. 1 cylinder, rotate the engine anticlockwise 180° until the TDC indent is at the bottom of the pulley. A temporary sticker positioned on the outer face of the crankshaft pulley will aid in finding the correct position for TDC on cylin-

Fig 2.27 Use a combination of screwdriver, ring spanner and feeler gauge to adjust both valve clearances on each cylinder. Most applications use 0.006in or 0.15mm.

Fig 2.28 It is useful to place a temporary sticker at TDC. Turn the engine 180° anticlockwise to adjust the valve clearances on cylinder no. 2. The sticker should be at the bottom when adjusting nos 2 and 4. Turn 180° again to adjust each cylinder in turn.

THE TYPE 1 ENGINE: KEEPING IT HEALTHY

Fig 2.29 Ensure that the cork gasket is a snug fit in the rocker box cover. Position the cover over the valve chest and lever the clip up until it clips into place.

ders 2 and 4. Cylinder no. 2 (right-hand rear) can now be checked and adjusted.
8. Rotate the engine 180° anticlockwise until the TDC indent is at the top of the pulley, where cylinder no. 3's (front left) valves can be checked.
9. Rotate the engine anticlockwise 180° again so the valves on cylinder no. 4 can be adjusted.
10. Renew the cork gaskets in the rocker covers and refit the covers by levering the spring retaining clip upwards with the large screwdriver until the clip clicks into the groove on the cover.
11. Run the engine and listen carefully for the sounds of a loose tappet, and check for oil leaks from the rocker covers before driving.

OIL FILTERS

The 1600cc CT unit used in the T3 Transporter, the Mexican Beetle equipped with fuel injection and all models that use the 1700, 1800 and 2-litre Type 4 engine also have a spin-on oil filter. These include the VW411 and 412 all the Transporters using the 1700, 1800 and 2-litre units, the Brazilian-built SP2 sports car and the VW/Porsche 914/4 models.

All Type 1 engines have an oil capacity of 2.5 litres. The exceptions are the suitcase-style CT engine used in the T3 Transporter and the fuel injection-equipped Mexican Beetle with the spin-on oil filter, which all have an oil capacity of 3 litres.

All applications using the Type 4 engine have an oil capacity of 3.5 litres when the spin filter is changed.

A suitable wrench will be required to remove the filter. There are several types, the most popular being a chain wrench or the type that fits over the filter and is driven by a ½in drive socket wrench. Lightly oil the sealing ring on the filter and tighten it into position by hand.

The Type 4 engine has a different arrangement for the oil strainer – just a single 8mm bolt in the centre of the strainer plate. The thread in the engine where this bolt locates is easily damaged so the bolt must only be tightened to 9lb ft (13Nm). The oil drain plug is located separate from the oil strainer and torque setting is 16lb ft (22Nm).

CHAPTER 3

ENGINE REMOVAL

To facilitate all repair procedures not covered in Chapter 2, it is advisable to remove the engine.

This chapter covers all models using the Type 1 unit, including the Beetle, Karmann Ghia, Type 181 Trekker, Fridolin post office van, Type 3 and Transporter models to the end of Bay Window production in 1979.

Tools required:
- Trolley jack
- Axle stands
- Large wooden blocks; 45cm lengths of railway sleeper are ideal
- Set of ring spanners, 8 to 22mm
- Medium flat-blade screwdriver
- Pliers or adjustable water pump pliers
- Pipe clamp
- A second trusted pair of hands

Although relatively light when compared with most car or light commercial vehicle engines, the Type 1 air-cooled unit is still heavy enough to cause injury if insufficient care is exercised when handling it. This is particularly true during removal and replacement, as this operation involves balancing the unit on the lifting plate of a trolley jack at full height. During removal, unless you are fortunate enough to have the use of a vehicle lift, the rear of the car will need to be lifted high enough for the engine and the trolley jack to be removed from under the rear valance and bumper bar.

The following procedures are primarily applicable to the Type 1 models (Beetle and Karmann Ghia). For operations specific to Transporter and Type 3, refer to the separate panels below.

LIFTING THE CAR (FIGS 3.1–3.2)

Only attempt the following method with the vehicle on firm, level ground. Remember, you are lifting the rear wheels off the ground, so putting the car in gear, with the handbrake on, will not prevent the vehicle from rolling. When the rear of the vehicle is raised it must be supported on axle stands under the rear torsion bar tubes. Before lifting, place suitable chocks forward of the front wheels only. This is to allow the car to roll back a little as the rear of the vehicle is raised. So long as you have confidence in the security and safety of axle stands under the torsion bar tubes, removing the rear wheels will improve access to the underbody. Bear in mind that engine removal can involve some pulling and shoving that will rock the vehicle, so the axle stands must be very steady and secure. Never use bricks or breeze blocks to support a vehicle; they can suddenly crumble, causing a serious accident to anyone unfortunate enough to be beneath the vehicle at the time.

As an additional safety measure, place wooden blocks and or the wheels and tyres under the jacking points, as a back-up in case the axle stands should topple.

1. Before attempting to remove the engine, disconnect the battery earth-strap. For easier access it may be desirable to remove the engine lid.
2. Raise the vehicle high enough to work underneath and to allow the engine and trolley jack to clear the rear valance.

    When raising the rear of the car, lift each side progressively and place the axle stand under

ENGINE REMOVAL

Fig 3.1 With the car supported on axle stands placed under the torsion bar tubes, the back should be sufficiently high for the engine to clear the rear valence.

the torsion bar tube before moving to the other side of the vehicle.

Move the axle stands up one peg at a time. If you are too greedy when lifting the car, the axle stand on the other side of the vehicle can tip, so be cautious. When the vehicle is high enough to clear the height of the engine and trolley jack, recheck the position of the chocks holding the front wheels and also place additional chocks behind the wheels.

3. If the engine is to be stripped down after removal it is much easier to drain the oil at this stage.

DISCONNECTING THE PIPEWORK (FIGS 3.3–3.8)

4. Next, crawl under the left side of the engine and remove the corrugated heater pipe that connects the left-hand heat exchanger/heater

Fig 3.2 The car should be raised progressively each side in turn, to prevent it from toppling. Also use blocks under the wheels before pulling the engine off the gearbox input shaft.

Fig 3.3 Under the car, disconnect the plastic heater tubes from the heat exchangers.

ENGINE REMOVAL

Fig 3.4 Under the car, clamp the fuel pipe and disconnect it from the pipe at the front of the engine. Securely plug the rubber pipe and release the clamp. On Transporters, always clamp the fuel pipe, as the fuel tank is above the engine.

Fig 3.6 Remove the rear lower tinware on the right of the engine, remove the 13mm screw from the thermostat and unscrew it from the rod.

box to the car's heater channel. Then clamp and plug the flexible fuel hose, having disconnected it from the metal pipe projecting from the front engine tinware.

5. Remove the corrugated pipe from the right-hand heat exchanger. If the engine is to be completely stripped down to its component parts, it is advisable to remove the thermostat at this stage. Using the flat-bladed screwdriver, undo and remove the screws holding the lower tinware panels between the heat exchangers and the crankcase.

6. Completely remove the lower right rear tinware plate; undo the 13mm bolt from the underside of the thermostat and unscrew it from the operating rod and away from its bracket.
7. Undo the 13mm bolt and remove the thermostat bracket. At this stage it's also a good idea to remove the screws holding both of the heat exchanger tinware shrouds to the crankcase.
8. Disconnect the heater flap clamps on the heat exchanger control levers from their respective cables.

Fig 3.5 Under the car, remove the screws attaching the heat exchangers to the lower tinware.

Fig 3.7 Remove the screws attaching the lower tinware to the crankcase.

ENGINE REMOVAL

Fig 3.8 Disconnect both heat exchanger control cables.

Fig 3.10 On post-1963 units, pull the short metal tubes from the exhaust box heater pods.

INSIDE THE ENGINE COMPARTMENT (FIGS 3.9–3.26)

9. For all engines from August 1964, first disconnect and remove the corrugated cardboard tubes between the fan housing and the rear tinware panel and, using pliers, pull the protruding metal tubes from the top of the heat exchanger connector pods on the exhaust box.
10. Remove the screws from the carburettor hotspot tube cover plates.
11. Remove the hot air feed pipe or pipes at the air filter assembly.

Fig 3.11 Remove the tinware pieces surrounding the carburettor hotspot tubes.

Fig 3.9 All units from August 1964, pull the short metal tubes from the exhaust box heater pods.

Fig 3.12 Disconnect the hot-air pipe or pipes from the air cleaner.

Fig 3.13 Remove the crankshaft pulley guard.

Fig 3.14 Remove the screws from the rear tinware and lift the panel clear of the engine bay.

Fig 3.15 Loosen the clamp holding the air-cleaner to the carburettor and remove the bolt holding the air filter bracket to the support bar.

Fig 3.16 1968 model year, carburettor pre-heating thermostatically controlled via a cable connected to a lever on the fan housing.

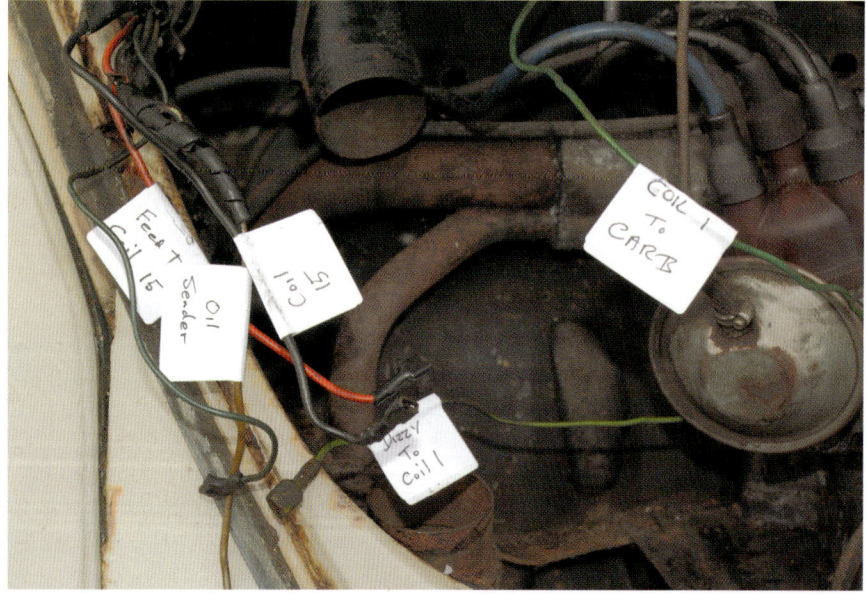

Fig 3.17 Label all the electrical connectors before disconnecting them from the engine components. Tuck the wiring loom out of the way.

12. Using the flat-bladed screwdriver, undo all the screws from the crankshaft pulley guard and the rear engine tinware panel and remove it from the engine bay.
13. Loosen the screw at the base of the air filter assembly and remove the screw from the support bracket if fitted. Lift off the air-cleaner and then cover the carburettor intake with a plastic bag or similar. Mark any vacuum hoses to aid reassembly. Some late 1960s models have a cable-operated flap connected to the thermostat linkage. This can be disconnected from the lever on the air-cleaner flap and the outer cable released after undoing the retaining screw.
14. Next, mark all electrical connections to the engine (masking tape makes good tags) to aid reassembly, then disconnect and tuck the loom out of the way. The connections include the oil pressure light sender unit situated on the left side of the engine just above the tinware, automatic choke and electromagnetic pilot jet on the carburettor and all connections to the alternator/generator or voltage regulator and the ignition coil.

SEMI-AUTOMATIC BEETLE

On semi-automatic Beetle and Karmann Ghia models only, disconnect the vacuum hose from the clutch solenoid at the top left-hand side of the engine compartment and tuck the pipe out of the way.

Also disconnect the auto-transmission fluid pipes leading from the dual oil-pump.

The torque converter must be separated from the drive plate on the engine before removing the engine mounting nuts and bolts. On these models a relatively thin drive plate is fitted instead of a flywheel. From under the vehicle the four bolts securing the torque converter to the drive plate are accessed through a hole in the side of the converter housing, just forward of the engine. The securing bolts have 8mm heads and it is recommended to use a single hexagonal socket or you are likely to round off the heads, making them almost impossible to remove. Slacken each bolt a little at a time before removing them to avoid distorting the drive plate.

Fig 3.18 On semi-automatic Type 1 vehicles disconnect the vacuum pipe from the clutch solenoid.

Fig 3.19 Disconnect the auto-transmission fluid pipes.

36 ENGINE REMOVAL

Fig 3.20 At the carburettor, release the accelerator cable from the throttle linkage.

Fig 3.21 Pull the accelerator cable guide tube from the fan housing.

15. Disconnect the accelerator cable at the carburettor and pull the guide tube from the fan housing.
    On 25 and 30PS models only, disconnect the choke cable at the carburettor. On most models the cable can now be pulled through the fan housing, though it is sometimes easier to wait until the engine has been pulled back prior to lowering it to the floor.
16. The engine is secured to the gearbox by just four points: two above, two below. The engine securing bolts have been altered over the years and have several variations. On models with the oil-cooler positioned forward of the fan housing on the left side of the engine, the upper-left mounting is a through-bolt screwed into a captive nut on the crankcase. This is accessed from under the vehicle and is quite fiddly to remove, requiring a 17mm socket, long extension bar and a ratchet wrench. Remove this one first, followed by the two 17mm nuts securing the lower mountings, also from under the car.
17. Now is a good time to have a willing helper to assist in lowering the engine. Ideally use a trolley jack with a high maximum lift to enable the engine to be lowered in one go. Place a trolley jack and, if needed, a block to make up the difference between the engine and trolley jack, under the oil strainer cover plate. The balance

Fig 3.22 On all 25 and 30PS models, remove the choke cable from the choke linkage.

Fig 3.23 Remove the two lower engine mounting nuts.

point is ideal if the jack and block are centred under the oil strainer plate. You may not be able to lower the engine to the floor in one go if you needed a block between the engine and the jack. In this case place two large blocks each side, in line with the heat exchangers, to rest the engine on.
18. Remove the 17mm nut from the right-hand top mounting bolt forward of the fan housing.
19. The gearbox driveshaft is easily damaged, so, with the helper holding the fan housing steady,

Fig 3.24 Two large wooden blocks (sleepers) are useful to rest the engine on before lowering to ground level. Any blocks between the jack and the engine can be removed at this point.

Fig 3.25 Having already removed the two lower nuts from the studs from under the vehicle, remove the two upper nuts. However, on later models with a captive nut in the crankcase at the top left, it is advisable to remove this bolt before the lower nuts. An early model is shown here.

pull the engine back until the release bearing contact plate, fitted to the clutch pressure plate on the early models, or the release fingers on the later clutch, clears the gearbox input shaft and the lower mounting studs are free from the holes in the gearbox. The exhaust system makes a good handle but make sure the tailpipes are secure if you have a standard system. Gently lower the engine, checking as you go that you are not damaging any components or the rubber surround. Don't forget to remove the accelerator cable from the fan housing if you left it in place earlier.
20. When the engine is safely on the two blocks, lower the jack and remove the packing block between the engine and the jack. Raise the jack under the strainer plate, remove the two blocks from under the heat exchangers, lower the unit to the floor and pull the engine clear from under the vehicle.

If you have the use of a ramp, complete all operations prior to pulling the engine back with the ramp raised, then lower the ramp, raise the jack under the strainer plate and pull the engine back to clear the gearbox shaft. Lower the engine and raise the ramp to enable the engine to be pulled clear under the rear valance. Early Transporter owners can place the jack under the engine and pull the whole unit back clear of the gearbox before lowering it to the floor.

Fig 3.26 Lower the engine and pull it clear of the vehicle.

ADDITIONAL PROCEDURES FOR TRANSPORTER MODELS USING THE TYPE 1 ENGINE

Transporters, including all Split Screen models and Bay Window vehicles up to August 1971, had a removable rear valance, enabling the engine to be removed with the wheels firmly on the ground, providing the suspension hasn't been lowered. With the Transporter's worldwide distribution this feature was useful in situations where garage facilities were few and far between. From August 1971, however, this useful feature was discarded in favour of a welded-in rear valance.

If you have a pre-August 1971 Transporter you may drive it onto ramps or tapered blocks.

Clamp the fuel hose before disconnecting it from the metal pipe protruding from the front tinware panel. This is important to remember on Transporter models where the fuel tank is higher than the engine. To prevent permanent crush damage to the flexible fuel hose, plug the end with a solid 6mm rod (a 6mm bolt is ideal for this) and tighten the pipe clip before releasing the clamp.

On Transporters built prior to August 1971, remove the rear bumper and undo the four set-screws holding the rear valance and integral rear tinware.

Remove the foam engine surround from post-1971 models.

Remove the air-cleaner and cover the carburettor intake with a plastic bag or similar, marking any vacuum hoses to aid reassembly. This is important, as on some Transporter models connecting the hoses incorrectly can lead to the manifold vacuum causing the fuel tank to collapse.

Remove the additional support bar holding the rear of the engine on second-generation Transporters. Early second-generation Transporters have no support for the rear of the gearbox, so you will need to rig up a means of preventing the gearbox from dropping after the engine has been removed. Transporters from the 1972 model year onwards have an additional cross-member supporting the rear of the gearbox from above, which negates the need for additional support when the engine is removed.

Fig 3.27 Transporters before August 1971 had a removable rear valance. The engine could be removed without raising the vehicle off its wheels providing it hadn't been lowered.

Fig 3.28 Transporters post 1971 used a foam surround to seal the engine compartment. It is important to check the condition regularly, as the foam can disintegrate and get sucked into the cooling fan, causing the engine to overheat.

Fig 3.29 When used in a Transporter, the rear of the Type 1 engine is supported by a bar attached to the chassis side members.

ADDITIONAL PROCEDURES FOR TYPE 3 MODELS

Remove the air-cleaner and cover the carburettor intakes with a plastic bag or similar, marking any vacuum hoses to aid reassembly.

Disconnect the accelerator cable from the twin carburettor linkage, or the intake air distributor on the fuel injection engine. Remove the additional support holding the rear of the engine. Although basically the same engine unit as the Type 1, the Type 3 has a flatter design of fan housing, connected to the air intake on the car body by a rubber bellows. The bellows can be removed after undoing the securing clips. Remove the dipstick and the rubber oil filler boot.

On the automatic, the torque converter must be separated from the drive plate on the engine before removing the engine-mounting nuts and bolts. On these models a relatively thin drive plate is fitted instead of a flywheel. From under the vehicle, the bolts securing the torque converter to the drive plate are accessed through a hole in the side of the converter housing, just forward of the engine. Slacken each bolt a little at a time before removing them to avoid distorting the drive plate.

TYPE 4 OR 2A ENGINES (FIGS 3.30–3.34)

This section covers all models using the Type 4 unit, including all 411 and 412 Type 4 vehicles and Type 2 Transporter models from August 1971 using developments of this engine, including the T25 or third generation Transporter, commonly known as the T3 up to 1982. This unit was also used in the Brazilian built SP2 sports car and the mid-engine VW-Porsche 914-4. The following procedures are primarily applicable to the Type 2 models (Bay Window Transporter). For additional operations specific to T3 Transporter, Type 4, 411 and 412 saloon and Variant models refer to separate panels. The tools required are the same as for Type 1 engines (*see* list at the start of this chapter).

This engine is a sturdier and therefore a much heavier lump than the Type 1 unit described above, so take care not to cause injury to yourself or an assistant during removal. This is particularly relevant for the home mechanic as the removal and replacement operation involves balancing the unit on the lifting plate of a trolley jack. During removal, unless you are fortunate enough to have the use of a vehicle lift, the rear of the car will need to be lifted high enough (but not as high as for the Type 1 unit) for the engine unit and the trolley jack to pass under the rear valance and bumper bar.

1. Before attempting to remove the engine, disconnect the battery leads. If the engine is to be completely dismantled after removal it is much easier to drain the oil at this stage.
2. Raise the vehicle high enough to work underneath and to allow the engine and trolley jack to clear the rear bodywork. Axle stands placed under the rear torsion bar tube should be used for support. When raising the rear of the Transporter, lift each side a little bit at a time, placing the axle stand under the torsion bar tube before moving to the other side of the vehicle. Lift progressively, moving the axle stand up one peg at a time. If you lift one side up too much, the axle stand on the other side of the vehicle can tip, so be cautious. When the vehicle is high enough, recheck the position of the chocks holding the front wheels and also place additional chocks behind the wheels.
3. Remove any hoses connected to the air-cleaner and remove the air-cleaner.
4. Disconnect the battery.
5. Label and disconnect all wiring to components fitted to the engine, including the alternator, oil pressure switch, ignition timing trigger, carburettors and temperature sensor. Disconnect

the wiring and hoses from the vacuum advance cut-off valve on dual-carburettor engines. On vehicles equipped with fuel injection, disconnect the wiring harness at the coil, the fuel injectors and the air intake distributor. An in-line fuse holder for the reversing lights is located near the coil and should be disconnected.
6. Remove the duct hoses connected to the heater blower.
7. Remove the ignition coil. Remove the hose and the left-hand hose connector from the left carburettor.
8. Disconnect the accelerator cable from the cross-rod on dual-carburettor engines or from the lever on the throttle valve on the fuel injection system.
9. Remove the foam engine surround, and the side and rear engine cover plates.
10. On the 1700, 1800 and 2-litre Type 4 engine, remove the dipstick and oil filler neck and disconnect the rubber joining hose at the bottom of the dipstick tube.

Fig 3.30 Remove the hoses connected to the heater blower.

Fig 3.31 The oil filler tube and dipstick tube rubber connector on 1700, 1800 and 2-litre Type 4 engines. The dipstick tube runs through the fan housing.

Fig 3.32 The two tubes connecting to the car heater system.

ENGINE REMOVAL

11. On automatic models with 1700, 1800 or 2-litre Type 4 engines only, pull out the ATF fluid dipstick and remove the filler pipe. Also remove the vacuum pipe from the intake air distributor, or, on dual-carburettor models, from the intake manifold balance pipe.
12. Remove the plug in the top left-hand corner of the front engine housing and remove the three bolts that connect the torque converter to the drive plate.
13. Disconnect the cables from the arms on the heat exchangers.

Fig 3.33 The tubes illustrated in Fig 3.32 connected to the Transporter heater tubes.

ADDITIONAL PROCEDURES FOR TYPE 4 411 AND 412 VARIANTS

On Type 4 Variant models, remove the louvred panel over the exhaust system to allow the engine to clear the bodywork. Support the car using axle stands under the rear axle carrier, forward of the rear suspension wishbones.

14. Pull off the ducts that connect the heat exchanger to the car's heater system.
15. Remove the two upper engine mounting bolts.
16. Rig up a means of supporting the transmission forward of the engine.
17. From under the car, pull the accelerator cable from its guide tube. Clamp and disconnect the fuel line at the front right of the engine.
18. Support the engine with a trolley jack and remove the lower engine mounting bolts.
19. Remove the bolts that connect the engine support bar to the chassis.
20. Pull the engine back until the gearbox input shaft clears the clutch or the torque converter clears the drive plate on automatic models.
21. Lower the engine to the floor.

Fig 3.34 From under the rear seat of a Type 4 Variant, remove the inspection cover, undo the nut and circlip on the gearbox input shaft and pull the shaft forward about 100mm (4in). The gearbox input shaft shown is removed from the gearbox for illustration purposes only.

ADDITIONAL PROCEDURES FOR THE T3 TRANSPORTER

Before attempting to remove the engine disconnect the battery earth strap. The battery is fitted under the right-hand front seat in most cases.

CHAPTER 4

REMOVING THE EXHAUST AND ANCILLARIES ON TYPE 1 ENGINES

Before the crankcase halves can be separated to examine and repair the internal components, the exhaust, ancillaries and tinware controlling the cooling airflow must be removed. Stand the engine on a suitable block so that only the crankcase is supported. It is also assumed that the oil has been drained before carrying out the following procedures.

Tools required:
- ⅜in or ½in drive socket set or ring spanners, 8 to 22mm
- 21mm and 30mm socket or ring spanner
- Flat-bladed screwdriver
- Telescopic magnet tool
- Long-nosed pliers

REMOVING THE FAN BELT AND FAN HOUSING (FIGS 4.1–4.6)

1. Using a flat-bladed screwdriver, remove the screws holding the front engine cover plate. (Refer to 4b4 and 4b5 for additional procedures on twin-port-head engines).
2. Remove the fan belt (*see* Chapter 2).
3. After marking the ignition leads to aid refitting, disconnect each plug cap from its spark plug and disconnect the leads from the clips on the fan housing. Unclip the distributor cap and remove the cap and leads. (*Refer* to page 45 for the procedure on 25 PS and 30 PS engines up to engine number 2 417 100).
4. Disconnect wires at the coil and the wire running to the distributor.
5. Remove the generator/alternator and fan housing as a unit. The procedure varies according to the year of manufacture.

Fig 4.1 *Undo the generator strap and slide it towards the fan housing.*

REMOVING THE EXHAUST AND ANCILLARIES ON TYPE 1 ENGINES

Fig 4.2 Remove the 6mm screws at each end of the fan housing using a flat-bladed screwdriver or 10mm spanner.

On all 25, 30 and 34PS engines up to July 1964 (1963 model year), engine number 8 796 622, proceed as follows:

1. Using a 13mm spanner, undo the bolt securing the strap holding the generator to its support bracket and slide the strap forward to clear the bracket.
2. Using the flat-bladed screwdriver (or occasionally a 10mm spanner), remove the two screws from each side of the fan housing.
3. Detach the spring from the throttle ring bracket forward of the fan housing and remove the two screws holding the ring to the bracket.
4. Lift the fan housing and generator clear, taking care not to damage the oil-cooler.

Fig 4.3 Unhook the spring and undo the two bolts holding the throttle ring and remove it from the fan housing.

Fig 4.4 Doghouse fan housing only: remove the four spring clips holding the connecting bar for the air deflection flaps, then unhook and remove the return spring. Remove the connecting bar.

Fig 4.5 Doghouse fan housing only: using a 10mm spanner, remove the bolt holding the upper air exit cover from the fan housing.

Fig 4.6 Use a 10mm spanner to remove the bolt holding the air outlet duct that exits through the front engine cover.

For engines from August 1964 (1965 model year) onwards, proceed as follows:

1. Only if the fan housing has a dog-leg cooler, perform the same operations as detailed in 5a1 and 5a2, and then remove the spring clips holding the connecting bar for the air deflection flaps in the fan housing. There is no need to remove the four screws holding each air deflection box to the fan housing.
2. Additionally, all twin-port-head, 1285cc, 44PS and 1584cc, 48PS and 50PS units produced after August 1970 are fitted with an external oil-cooler forward of the fan housing, commonly known as a 'doghouse' oil-cooler. These units have an additional oil-cooler cover and an air exit duct that passes through the front engine cover plate and can be removed by undoing the 10mm-headed set screws holding them in place.
3. After checking that the thermostat has been unscrewed from its control rod under the right-hand side of the engine, the fan housing and generator/alternator may be lifted clear of the engine.

REMOVE THE FUEL PUMP (FIGS 4.7–4.8)

1. On 25PS and 30PS engines, undo the pipe unions and remove the metal fuel pipes from both the fuel pump and the carburettor. Remove the nuts securing the fuel pump to the side of the crankcase. Remove the pushrod and the plastic intermediate flange from the crankcase.
2. On all other Type 1 engines, the fuel pump is mounted on top of the crankcase and is connected to the carburettor and the metal fuel inlet pipe with flexible rubber fuel hoses secured with pipe clips. Remove the pushrod and the intermediate flange from the crankcase.

REMOVING THE EXHAUST AND ANCILLARIES ON TYPE 1 ENGINES

Fig 4.7 Undo the two metal pipe unions to the fuel pump on 25 and 30PS engines. Undo the two 13mm nuts, remove the side-mounted pump, the operating rod and the plastic intermediate flange.

Fig 4.8 All 30PS Transporter engines from 1959, 34PS and later engines have flexible rubber fuel pipes with pipe clips to fasten them to the fuel pump. This type of pump is mounted on the top of the crankcase. Remove the pump, the operating rod and the plastic intermediate flange. The plastic flange is often a very tight fit in the case and is known to break. The only remedy is to break up the plastic when the case has been opened.

REMOVE INLET MANIFOLD (FIGS 4.9–4.14)

Remove the inlet manifold with the carburettor. The 25PS and 30PS engines employ an additional tube to carry the ignition leads, which is positioned above the manifold and held by the means of screw-mounted clips. This feature was discontinued from chassis number 2 417 101.

1. When removing the manifold on the engines equipped with this tube, unclip the distributor cap and remove the plug caps from the spark plugs, having marked the leads to aid refitting. Remove the screws securing the two clips that hold the tube to the fan housing.

Fig 4.9 All 25 and 30PS engines to engine number 2 417 101 are fitted with a tube connected to the fan housing to protect the ignition leads. Label and remove the ignition leads from the spark plugs, remove the tube from the fan housing, unclip the distributor cap and remove from the engine. On all other engines, label and remove the ignition leads from the spark plugs and remove distributor cap.

46 REMOVING THE EXHAUST AND ANCILLARIES ON TYPE 1 ENGINES

Fig 4.10 Remove the 13mm nut holding the carburettor bracing strut from the crankcase.

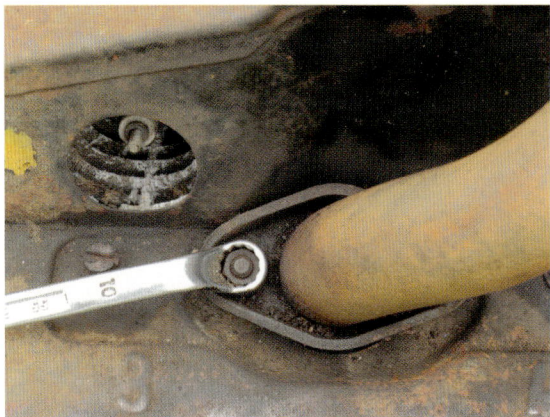

Fig 4.11 Remove the 10mm nuts holding the inlet manifold to the cylinder head.

Fig 4.12 Remove the 10mm bolts holding the inlet manifold hotspot tube to the exhaust box.

Fig 4.13 The three-piece twin-port inlet manifold is bolted to the cylinder head with 13mm nuts.

2. The carburettor only needs to be separated from the manifold if it is being serviced or repaired. Some models have a bracing strut between the rear carburettor-mounting stud and the engine. Remove the lower nut holding the brace.
3. For all other engines to July 1970 and all single-port engines thereafter, a 10mm cranked ring spanner is all that is required to remove the manifold. Undo two nuts for each inlet port and two for each side on the connection between the carburettor heater tube and the exhaust box.
4. All twin-port-head engines require a 13mm ring spanner to remove the nuts at the inlet ports. Use a 10mm spanner for the connection to the carburettor hotspot tube at the exhaust box. You will also need a Phillips screwdriver to slacken the clips surrounding the rubber joining sleeves that connect the three sections of the manifold.

REMOVING THE EXHAUST AND ANCILLARIES ON TYPE 1 ENGINES 47

Fig 4.14 The three sections of the twin-port manifold are joined with rubber connectors held in place with pipe clips.

REMOVING TWIN-PORT INLET MANIFOLD NUTS

Top tip: use a ½in AF ring spanner, which is a tight fit on these 13mm nuts, to avoid slipping and rounding the corners.

Note that the early 34PS engines may have been converted to the later system during the life of the car. The upper exhaust mounting flange is secured to the rear exhaust ports on the cylinder head with 13mm nuts on all versions of the Type 1 engine.

Depending on the model and year of manufacture, tubes known as warm air elbows are in

REMOVE THE EXHAUST SYSTEM (FIGS 4.15–4.18)

1. Assuming the inlet manifold has been disconnected from the top surface of the rear exhaust flanges, the next job is to undo and remove the flange clips connecting the heater boxes on engines to 3 949 282 (30PS) or 7 336 419 (34PS), or the heat exchangers on all subsequent engines, to the lower tubes on the silencer.

Fig 4.16 The warm air elbow is fitted to right-hand exhaust box flange for carburettor pre-heating on this 1967 44PS 1500.

Fig 4.17 This later example of a warm-air elbow was fitted to collect warm air from under no. 2 cylinder for carburettor pre-heating from July 1968 onwards. It is fastened to the cylinder shroud and lower rear tinware.

Fig 4.15 After the inlet manifold hotspot bolts have been removed, there are two 13mm nuts holding the exhaust box to each cylinder head.

48 REMOVING THE EXHAUST AND ANCILLARIES ON TYPE 1 ENGINES

Fig 4.18 Remove the 13mm nuts holding the heat exchanger to the front exhaust port on the cylinder head.

Fig 4.19 Using a flat-bladed screwdriver, remove the screws holding the cylinder covers to the cylinder heads.

Fig 4.20 If reusing the clutch, undo the 13mm bolts a little at a time to avoid distorting the clutch pressure plate.

some cases attached to the studs on the rear exhaust flanges. Keep these safe ready to reinstall later, as they are an important component, supplying warm air to the carburettor during warm-up.

2. Remove the heater boxes on 25PS/30PS and early 34PS engines or heat exchangers on 34PS ones from engine number 7 336 420 and all later units.

If you haven't already done so, use a flat-bladed screwdriver to remove the lower screws holding the curved tinware between the heat exchanger and the crankcase. Using the 13mm spanner or socket remove the nuts holding the heat exchangers to the front exhaust-port flange on the cylinder head. The heat exchanger may then be lifted off the front exhaust studs and away from the engine.

REMOVE UPPER CYLINDER COVERS

Using a flat-bladed screwdriver, remove the screws securing the upper cylinder covers to the cylinder heads. (Fig 4.19)

REMOVE THE CLUTCH ASSEMBLY

With the flywheel stopped from turning with a suitable locking device, use a 13mm socket or spanner and slacken each screw holding the clutch pressure plate to the flywheel. Carry on slackening each screw a little at a time to avoid distorting the pressure plate if it's to be reused; however, unless the clutch is very new, it's advisable to replace the complete clutch now, rather than having to remove the rebuilt engine unnecessarily at a later date. (Fig 4.20)

REMOVE DISTRIBUTOR

Use a 13mm spanner to remove the single nut and remove the distributor. Use long-nosed pliers or a thin screwdriver to remove the anti-chatter spring out of the top of the distributor driveshaft and bag it with the distributor. For distributor driveshaft removal, *see* Chapter 5. (Figs 4.21–4.22)

REMOVING THE EXHAUST AND ANCILLARIES ON TYPE 1 ENGINES 49

Fig 4.21 Remove the single 13mm nut securing the distributor bracket to the crankcase and remove the distributor.

Fig 4.22 Use long-nosed pliers to remove the anti-chatter spring from the centre of the distributor driveshaft.

Fig 4.23 Remove the three 10mm nuts securing the oil-cooler to the crankcase. Discard the rubber seals.

REMOVE OIL COOLER

Using a 10mm spanner, remove the three nuts holding the oil-cooler to the crankcase. On the twin-port engine you may remove the oil-cooler complete with the intermediate mounting bracket. (Fig 4.23)

CLEAN THE CRANKCASE

Block all the entry points into the engine and, using a suitable engine degreasing fluid, thoroughly clean all the dirt and grease from the unit.

At this stage you may have decided not to delve into the internals of the engine. If this proves to be the case, you needn't proceed any further, as the unit as it stands is what you trade in if you opt for a replacement engine. Be aware that some suppliers sell engines without the distributor driveshaft.

REMOVE OIL STRAINER COVER PLATE

Tip the engine flywheel end down and, using a 10mm socket, remove the six nuts surrounding the oil drain plug from beneath the engine and remove the cover plate and oil strainer. Some later engines didn't have a drain plug, just a cover plate to retain the oil strainer (*see* Chapter 2).

REMOVE OIL PRESSURE AND OIL CONTROL VALVES (FIG 4.24)

Having cleaned all the oil and dirt from the case with an engine degreasing liquid, remove the oil pressure relief valve and, on later engines, the oil control valve.

These are situated on the underside of the left-hand case half and have large slotted covers that are too wide for most screwdrivers. All units have the oil pressure relief valve at the rear of the case, while later engines also have an oil control valve at the front. Remove the relief valve caps, followed by a large spring and the relief valve piston. Bag up and mark each set, as they must be returned to their original locations.

Fig 4.24 With the engine tipped forward onto the flywheel end, use a wide-bladed screwdriver to undo the oil pressure relief valve plug and, if fitted, the oil control valve plug. Withdraw the spring and piston, label and bag to aid refitting. The oil pressure relief valve is the one at the pulley end of the case.

CHAPTER 5

ENGINE STRIP-DOWN

For the final strip-down it is advisable to have a collection of containers and bags to hand for storing components. Plastic moneybags from a bank are useful for small components. Carefully label components as you remove them.

REMOVING THE CRANKSHAFT/ GENERATOR PULLEY – TYPE 1 ENGINE (FIGS 5.1–5.4)

1. Fit a flywheel-locking tool to prevent the flywheel from turning and undo the 30mm bolt holding the generator pulley to the crankshaft. With the bolt removed you may be able to wriggle the pulley off, but usually a puller is required.

Fig 5.2 With a flywheel-locking tool in place, the clutch and crankshaft pulley can be removed. This is not recommended for removing the high-torque flywheel-retaining bolt.

Fig 5.1 With the flywheel locked in position (see Fig 5.6), use a 30mm spanner to undo the pulley bolt.

ENGINE STRIP-DOWN

Fig 5.4 Remove the two screws holding the inner pulley guard.

2. With the pulley removed from the engine, take off the inner pulley cover, having removed all screws securing it to the engine and lower tinware deflector plates.

REMOVING THE FLYWHEEL (FIGS 5.5–5.8A)

For those planning to uprate a 6-volt engine to 12-volt, it is worth noting that the flywheel on engines equipped with a 6-volt electrical system differs from the one fitted to 12-volt units. The 6-volt flywheel has 109 teeth and the 12-volt flywheel has 130 teeth, thus presenting problems with the starter motor. Although this is not recommended, many owners risk running 12 volts through a 6-volt starter motor. The exception to this compatibility rule is the 6-volt cars produced in the 1967 model year, identified by still having sloping headlights (except cars destined for the US market, which were equipped with the upright headlights usually associated with 1968 model year cars for all other markets). The 1967 model year cars were equipped with the same 130-tooth flywheel used on all 12-volt cars. The two types of flywheel are not interchangeable as they are different where they attach to the crankshaft.

MAKING A PULLER

This can be manufactured locally using a length of metal bar with a central threaded hole and two holes to align with the two holes in the pulley. Two long bolts with a means of gripping the pulley are then threaded through the holes in the pulley, and when the central bolt is tightened, the pulley is pulled clear of the crankshaft. Take care not to damage the internal thread in the crankshaft.

Fig 5.3 When the crankshaft pulley is tight on the shaft a puller may be needed to remove it. A locally made device is illustrated here.

ENGINE STRIP-DOWN

Fig 5.5 With the flywheel lock in place, the six 13mm-headed bolts holding the clutch may be removed.

1. Volkswagen technicians used a flywheel-locking tool when removing the flywheel, but now some specialists claim that using one may cause the crankcase to crack when force is exerted to undo the nut. Instead, make your own locking device using a 1.2m (4ft) length of sturdy angle iron. Drill two 8mm holes with the centres to align with the holes on two of the clutch-retaining bolt holes on the flywheel. Using two of the clutch screws, bolt the bar to the flywheel before attempting to undo the flywheel nut.

2. With the flywheel-locking tool or DIY angle iron tool bolted in place, position the engine on a hard surface at ground level with the length of angle iron supported on suitable blocks, or in a free-standing bench vice to prevent the unit from tipping. Position the 36mm socket on the flywheel nut and, using suitable force, undo and remove the nut. With the nut removed, wriggle the flywheel off the four locating dowels fitted into the crankshaft, taking care not to drop it and crush your fingers when it comes free of the dowels, as it is surprisingly heavy.

The flywheel is bolted up extremely tight (217lb ft or 294Nm), so only use suitable tools to remove the securing nut. Use at least a ¾in sliding T-bar with a 36mm socket. It may be necessary to extend the bar with a suitable length of steel tubing. An assistant may also be required to hold the engine securely while the nut is undone.

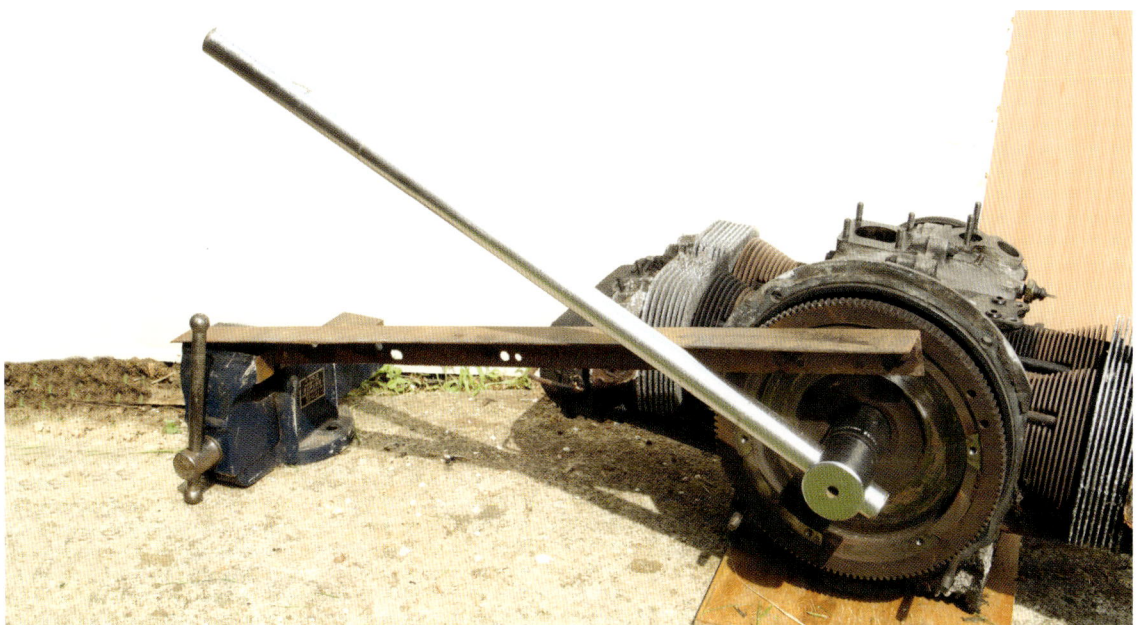

Fig 5.6 A length of angle iron bolted to the flywheel and supported by blocks or a free-standing bench vice is a stable set-up for removing the high-torque flywheel retaining bolt.

REMOVING THE FYWHEEL ON 1700, 1800 AND 2-LITRE TYPE 4 ENGINES

Fit a flywheel-locking device. Before removing the flywheel, undo the central bolt on the fan hub at the rear of the engine.

To remove the fan hub, slide metal packing pieces between the three fan bolt holes and the crankcase. Screw three long 8mm threaded bolts into the holes in the fan hub and tighten to remove the hub from the crankshaft. Remove the Woodruff key from the crankshaft. The flywheel is connected to the crankshaft with five bolts. Undo the five bolts and remove the five-holed bolt plate and the flywheel.

The flywheel is located on the crankshaft with a rolled pin; this may need to be removed if further work is to be carried out on the crankshaft. Remove the O-ring from the groove in the nose of the flywheel.

The bearing for the gearbox input shaft is in the end of the crankshaft. To remove the bearing, pack it with grease and insert a gearbox input shaft. A few taps with a hammer should extract the bearing using hydraulic pressure.

Fig 5.7 To remove the fan hub on 1700, 1800 and 2-litre engines, first remove the 13mm-headed central bolt. Place metal packing pieces behind the three bolt holes for the fan. Screw in three long 8mm threaded bolts and tighten to extract the fan hub from the crankshaft.

Fig 5.8 Remove the five 17mm headed bolts securing the flywheel on 1700, 1800 and 2-litre Type 4 engines. Discard the five-holed bolt plate.

Fig 5.8A The bearing that supports the gearbox input shaft is mounted in the end of the crankshaft on 1700, 1800 and 2-litre Type 4 engines. A new bearing is illustrated; it should be installed with the felt ring nearest the end of the crankshaft.

ENGINE STRIP-DOWN

DISTRIBUTOR DRIVESHAFT (FIG 5.9)

A special tool is available for the removal of the shaft, but a suitably whittled piece of wood forced into the indentation in the top of the shaft can be just as effective. Using a pair of long-nosed pliers, remove the spring from the indentation on the top of the shaft, then tap the wooden tool into the indentation on the top of the distributor driveshaft and lift it out while turning it anticlockwise. Using a suitable telescopic magnet, retrieve the two washers that the shaft sat on at the base of the hole and bag them for use on reassembly. Alternatively, if you are dismantling the engine completely, remove the shaft and washers when the two case halves are separated.

REMOVING THE OIL PUMP (FIGS 5.10–5.11)

Using a 10mm spanner or socket on early engines, or a 13mm one on later units, remove the four oil pump-retaining nuts, situated at the pulley end of the engine.

Lift off the pump cover plate and then remove the pump gears and bag them for use later, unless you intend to replace the whole pump. Auto stick-shift models have a double pump with an intermediate flange separating the two elements of the pump. The outer gears control the flow of the automatic transmission fluid (ATF) to the torque converter.

The body of the pump can now be wriggled off the four studs. It may appear to be stuck but do not use a tool between the case and the pump body as the mating surfaces will be damaged. There is a special puller made for this operation that hooks into the body of the pump. As a last resort, remove the pump body later, after the case halves have been separated. To facilitate this, remove the oil pump studs from the right-hand case half.

Fig 5.9 A whittled wooden peg can be used to remove the distributor driveshaft as long as the shaft isn't too tight in its crankcase bore.

Fig 5.10 Remove the four 10mm nuts holding the oil pump cover. Later engines from 1967 onwards used 13mm nuts.

Fig 5.11 Remove and bag the oil pump gears. Auto stick-shift models have a double pump, with an intermediate flange between the engine oil pump and the outer set of gears used to drive the auto transmission fluid pump.

REMOVING STUDS

Top tip: studs can be removed by locking two nuts together on the stud and positioning the spanner on the inner nut to unscrew the stud from the engine case. Position the spanner on the outer nut to re-install the stud.

Fig 5.12 If the pump body is tight in the crankcase, don't try to force it by prying between the flange and the case, as it will damage the mating surfaces and leak when refitted. Remove the two studs from the right-hand case-half by locking two nuts together.

Fig 5.13 When the nuts are locked together, turn the inner nut anticlockwise to unscrew the stud from the case. Apply the spanner to the outer nut when refitting the studs.

REMOVING THE CYLINDER HEADS (FIGS 5.14–5.20)

While the cylinder heads are still secured to the engine case, it is advisable to remove the spark plugs.

1. Remove the rocker box covers by inserting a large screwdriver between the spring clip and the cover from above, before levering downwards to release the clip.
2. Pull off the rocker box cover and discard the cork gasket.

Fig 5.14 Lever the rocker box cover clip downwards to remove the cover.

ABOVE: Fig 5.15 Remove and discard the rocker cover gasket.

Fig 5.16 Remove the two 13mm nuts holding each rocker shaft. The 1700, 1800 and 2-litre Type 4 engines have two shafts per head, secured with 11mm nuts.

ENGINE STRIP-DOWN

Fig 5.17 Remove the pushrods.

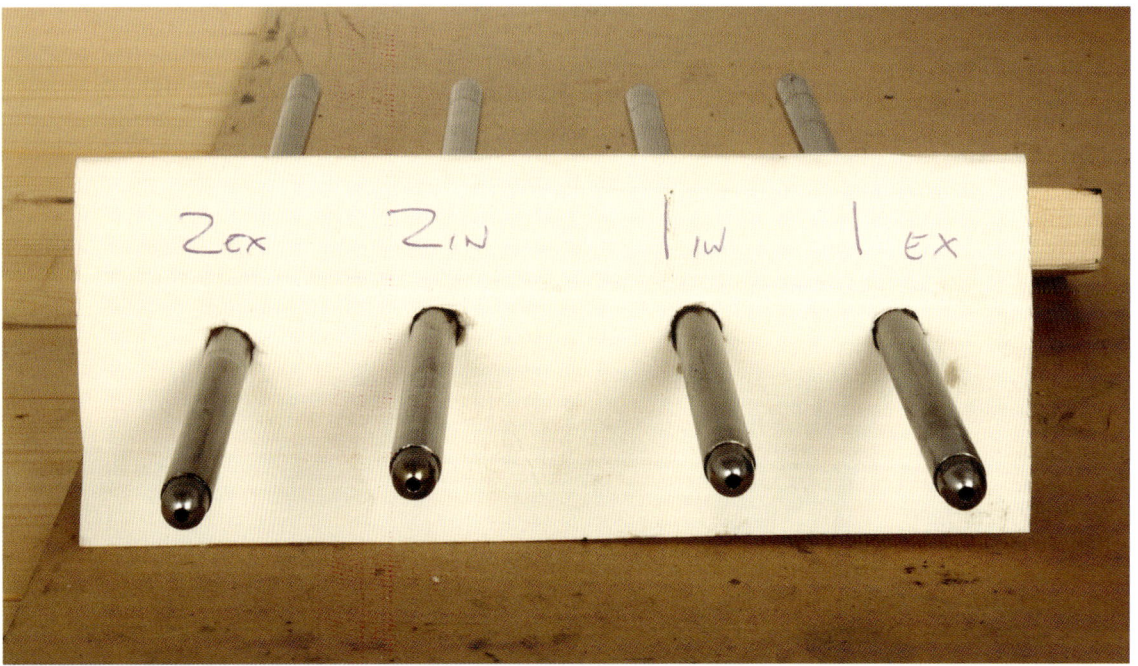

Fig 5.18 Mark the pushrod locations on two pieces of card and push the removed rods through the card.

ENGINE STRIP-DOWN 59

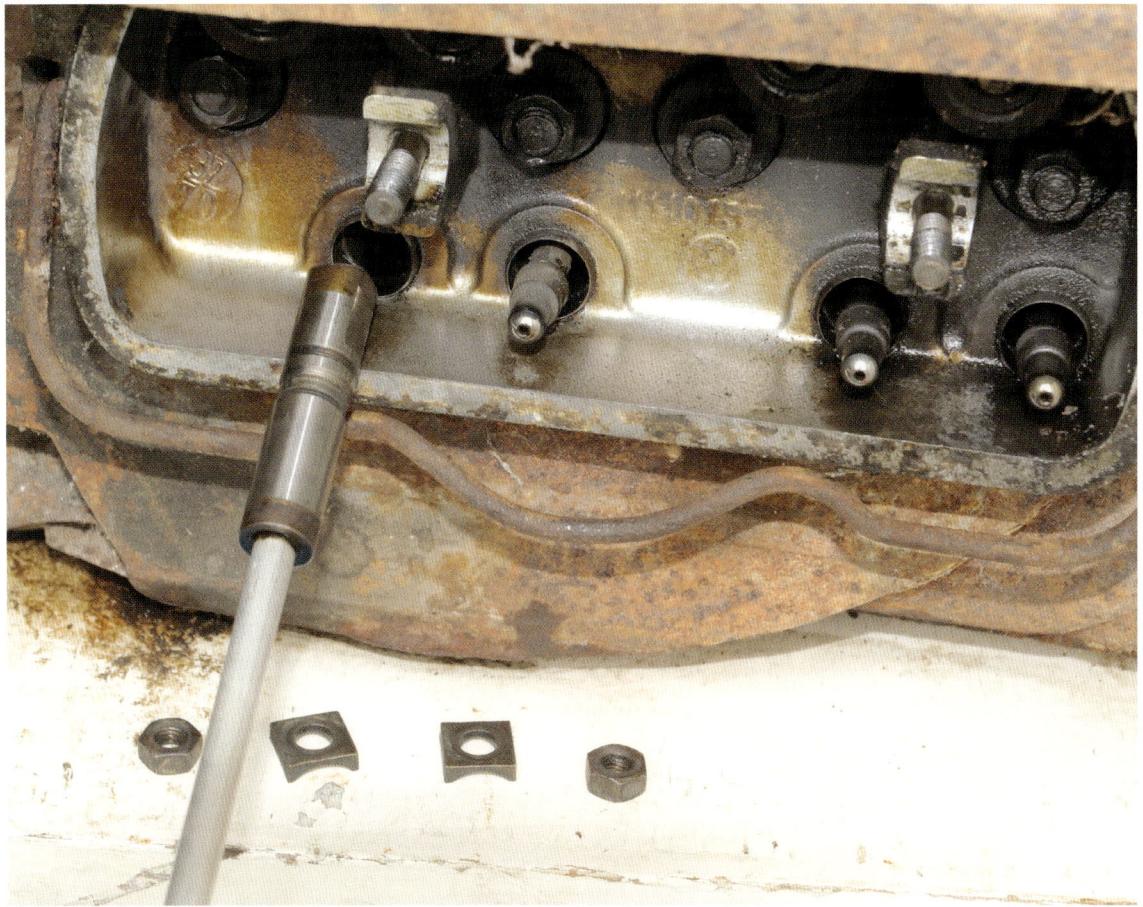

Fig 5.18A The cam follower and pushrod is an integral unit on 25 and 30PS engines.

3. Using a 13mm spanner, undo the two nuts holding the rocker shaft and lift the shaft off the studs.
4. Repeat the last two operations for the other head. The two rocker shafts per cylinder head fitted to 1700, 1800 and 2-litre Type 4 engines are secured with 11mm nuts.
5. Next take two pieces of card and make four holes in each and write the valve position on each card. Pull the pushrods from their respective positions and push them through the cards.
6. The cam followers on 25 and 30PS units are attached to the pushrod and are removed at this stage. Metal plates within the crankcase prevent them from turning. Keep them safe, pushed through a numbered card.

7. Referring to Fig 5.19, undo each head nut one flat at a time, in reverse order, using a 15mm socket. Undoing each nut in this manner helps to reduce the possibility of distorting the cylinder heads. Keep returning to each nut in sequence until they are loose enough to undo by hand. Retain the nuts and washers for use during reassembly.
8. Lift the cylinder heads off the studs, taking care not to pull the cylinder barrels with them. Once the cylinder head has been detached from the studs, the pushrod tubes (positioned between the head and the crankcase) may be removed and placed to one side for when the engine is reassembled. However, they do rust and as they are cheap to replace you may feel they are not worth keeping.

ENGINE STRIP-DOWN

Fig 5.19 Cylinder head-tightening diagram. Loosen the cylinder head nuts in small increments to prevent the head from distorting. Loosen in the reverse order to the sequence shown.

Fig 5.20 With the head loosened, remove the pushrod tubes and discard the rubber sealing rings.

REMOVING THE CYLINDER BARRELS

For peace of mind, it is advisable to replace the pistons and barrels with new parts. However, if you are intending to reuse them, mark the cylinders with paint or Tipp-Ex to help you replace them into their original positions.

Slide the barrels off the studs and remove the paper gasket from the mating surfaces with the crankcase.

REMOVING THE PISTONS (FIGS 5.21–5.22)

1. Using suitable long-nose pliers, remove the circlips from each side of the piston pin.
2. The pistons are a tight interference fit to the piston pin (gudgeon pin) and require heating to allow the pin to be removed. Place a suitable bowl under the piston to be worked on and pour boiling water over the piston; then, working quickly, push the pin out using a suitable drift. When rotating the crankshaft to find the top dead centre position for piston pin removal, make sure that the other connecting rods and piston skirts are not binding against the apertures in the case.

1700, 1800 AND 2-LITRE TYPE 4 ENGINES

After the pushrods have been removed the pushrod tubes may be extracted from the cylinder head. Unhook the spring clip from inside the rocker box and pull the pushrod tubes through the holes in the rocker box using a twisting motion.

ENGINE STRIP-DOWN

Fig 5.21 Remove the piston pin retaining circlips.

Fig 5.22 Quickly remove the heated gudgeon pin with a suitable drift. Work on the pistons that are at the top of their stroke.

REMOVING THE GENERATOR SUPPORT (FIG 5.23)

This applies to 34PS and later Type 1 engines only. Using the 13mm spanner, remove the four nuts holding the oil filler/generator support and lift it clear of the crankcase (on all engines except the 25 and 30PS, units where this feature is integral with the case). There is one exception; the 30PS Transporter engine from the 1959 model year also had a removable generator support.

SEPARATING THE CRANKCASE HALVES (FIGS 5.24–5.29)

Tools required:
- 13mm socket/spanner
- 17mm socket/spanner

Before attempting to separate the crankcase halves it is essential to have removed the flywheel, pulley or fan hub on Type 4 engines, as detailed at the start of this chapter. The engine must be tipped onto its left side, with connecting rods 1 and 2 pointing upwards and the whole unit supported between blocks, or suspended between the jaws of a workmate-type portable bench.

Fig 5.23 Undo the four 13mm nuts and remove the generator support. Discard the gaskets and the metal baffle.

1. When the upper case half is lifted clear the cam followers will fall out, unless you have some special clips to hold them in place.
2. Using the 13mm socket remove the smaller nuts first, before moving onto the 17mm nuts. Two of the smaller fastenings are nut and bolt, the rest are studs and nuts.

Fig 5.24 With all the pistons removed, tilt the crankcase onto its left side with the connecting rods for cylinders 1 and 2 facing up. Place between blocks or the jaws of a portable workbench. You will need a small block to level it up. If available, use clips to retain the cam followers in the right-hand case half.

Fig 5.25 Undo all the small nuts and bolts first.

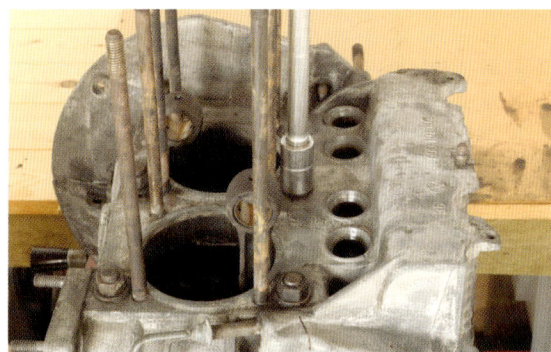

Fig 5.26 Remove the six larger nuts. A sealing compound is used between the crankcase halves, so you may need to suspend the engine using the head studs to support the engine a centimetre or so above the workbench or blocks. Use a length of batten and hammer to tap on the case flanges until a gap begins to open.

3. With all the nuts and bolts removed, the upper case half may be lifted clear. When the engine is assembled the case flanges are coated with a gasket sealant, which may cause difficulty when trying to separate the two halves. Do not pry anything between the flanges as this may cause an oil leak when reassembled. With the crankcase suspended, tap the protruding flanges on the lower half with a plastic mallet or hammer on a length of wood. Do not hit the case too hard or use a hammer directly on the flanges. Gradually a gap will open up between the flanges, enabling the oil pump body to be removed. Lift the right-hand case-half clear.

Fig 5.27 When the gap between the case halves opens, the oil pump body is released, providing the studs have been removed from the right-hand case half.

ENGINE STRIP-DOWN

Fig 5.28 Eventually the left-hand case half, containing the crankshaft and camshaft, will drop. Lift the right-hand case-half clear.

Fig 5.29 Remove and bag the plug at the flywheel end of the camshaft.

Fig 5.30 Remove the camshaft, the camshaft bearings where fitted and the sealing rings around the six studs.

4. Remove the small circular plug that sits in line with the camshaft from the flywheel end of the case.

REMOVING THE CAMSHAFT (FIG 5.30)

The camshaft is gear-driven from the crankshaft and may be lifted clear by lifting the shaft and rotating it around the crankshaft gear. The camshaft bearing shells from all 34PS and larger engines may now be removed from the crankcase halves. (The earlier 25 and 30PS engines didn't have removable camshaft bearing shells; instead the camshaft ran directly on the bearing surfaces in the crankcase.)

Remove the O-ring seals from the six large crankcase studs.

REMOVING AND STRIPPING DOWN THE CRANKSHAFT ASSEMBLY (FIGS 5.31–5.40)

1. Before removing the crankshaft, pry the oil seal from the flywheel end of the crankcase, taking care not to damage the seat in the case. Grasp the two uppermost connecting rods and lift the assembly clear of the crankcase half and place it on a clean surface.
2. The centre no. 2 main bearing shells can now be removed from the crankcase halves. Remove and bag all the main bearing location dowels.
3. The crankshaft is supported by four main bearings, three of which are circular one-piece bear-

Fig 5.31   Grasp the connecting rods and lift the crankshaft clear of the case.

Fig 5.32   Remove the split no. 2 main bearing shells from the case halves. Remove and bag all the main bearing dowels from the case. Remove all the cam followers.

Fig 5.33   Remove and bag the crankshaft end-float shims and remove the circular no. 1 bearing shell.

SAFETY

In the interest of fire safety, remove all flammable liquids and components such as fuel pump and carburettor well away from the work area before lighting a blowlamp.

Fig 5.34   Remove the Woodruff key from the keyway at the pulley end of the crankshaft.

ings: no. 1 may be slid off the crankshaft at the flywheel end, along with the end-float shims. No. 2, as already mentioned, is the split type and each half remains in the case halves.

4. Bearing nos 3 and 4 can only be removed after more work to the crankshaft. From the pulley end of the crankshaft remove the Woodruff key followed by the concave oil deflector disc. At this point no. 4 main bearing may be removed from the crankshaft.

ENGINE STRIP-DOWN

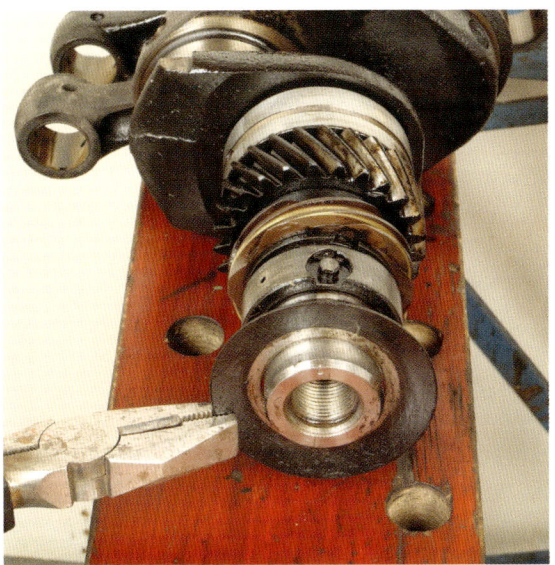

Fig 5.35 Remove the concave oil deflector disc.

Fig 5.36 Remove the circular no. 4 main-bearing shell.

5. Screw the flywheel bolt into the crankshaft and stand the assembly upright in a vice. Remove the nuts holding the connecting rods; remove the rods from the crankshaft and, using a small flat-bladed screwdriver, pry the bearing shells from the rod and bearing cap.

Fig 5.37 Screw the flywheel-retaining bolt into the crankshaft and stand the assembly in a vice. Remove all the connecting rods.

Fig 5.38 The connecting rods with big end bearing shells removed, gear-retaining circlip, Woodruff key and oil thrower disc.

ENGINE STRIP-DOWN

Fig 5.39 Using flat-bladed circlip pliers, remove the gear-retaining circlip.

Fig 5.40 Use a suitable puller to remove the two gears and spacer from the crankshaft. Remove the circular no. 3 main-bearing shell.

6. Next, using suitable circlip pliers, remove the gear-retaining circlip followed by the distributor drive gear. The common types of circlip pliers with pointed ends are not suitable for this application. Instead use the circlip pliers with flattened ends that grip the ends of the circlip and expand outwards.

7. Position a suitable puller (*see* below) with the fingers behind the camshaft drive gear, heat the gear with boiling water or a blowtorch to expand it, and wind up the puller to remove the gears off the crankshaft. The spacer between the distributor drive gear and the camshaft drive gear may now be removed.

   Use of a conventional gear puller will almost certainly damage the gear, requiring use of a new gear on reassembly. *Refer* to next paragraph.

8. Those with access to a hydraulic press may remove the gears and spacer from the crankshaft after removing the circlip holding the camshaft gear and the distributor drive gear. In this case, position the support plate under the camshaft drive gear and apply the ram pressure to the end of the crankshaft. With the gears removed, the circular no. 3 main bearing may be removed from the crankshaft. (Fig 5.40)

CYLINDER HEAD STRIP-DOWN (FIGS 5.41–5.44)

Tools required:
- Valve spring compressor with sufficient depth to clear the rim of the valve chest
- Long-nose pliers and/or thin screwdriver

1. Position the valve spring compressor with the static jaw on the valve head and the moveable jaw on the valve spring retainer. Compress the valve spring and, using the screwdriver, dislodge the valve collets from the stem of the valve. Use long-nose pliers or a magnet to retrieve the collets.

2. Release the spring compressor and remove the valve spring and retainer.

ENGINE STRIP-DOWN

Fig 5.41 Valve spring compressor. This one has deep enough jaws to clear the edge of the valve chest.

Fig 5.42 With the valve spring compressed, use a magnet to retrieve the valve collets.

3. Push the valve through the valve guide and remove from the cylinder head. Bag and label each valve, along with the spring, collets and retainer as you remove them.
4. The rocker shafts, removed earlier, may be further dismantled. Remove the circlip at the end of the shaft and pull off and lay out the components in the order that you removed them.

Fig 5.43 Remove the valve spring and valve keeper.

Fig 5.44 Exploded view of the rocker shaft components. This one is from a 30PS engine; later models are similar but with detail differences.

CHAPTER 6

EXAMINATION OF THE ENGINE COMPONENTS

CRANKCASE

If the engine was covered in oil prior to removal, this could be due to a number of reasons:

- Exhaust gases entering the crankcase by bypassing the pistons and/or rings and pressurizing the crankcase, therefore causing oil to exude from the crankcase breather or from where the pulley is attached at the rear of the crankshaft, or any other suitable orifice
- The seals between the oil-cooler and crankcase having failed
- The front crankshaft oil seal at the flywheel having failed
- The maximum oil level having been exceeded; again, this would exude from the pulley end of the crankcase
- The crankcase having split

If you suspect the crankcase has split, take it to a local friendly garage and ask to use the parts washer for a final clean. Having cleaned off all the dirt, thoroughly examine each case half for cracks. If you suspect a crack, heat applied for a few seconds will open it up long enough for you to detect it. It is more likely to be on the left half of the case as the main oil gallery runs between the oil-cooler and the oil pressure sensor. A crack between the oil pressure sender hole and the top rear cylinder head stud is relatively common, as is a crack in the bell housing next to no. 3 cylinder. Also check inside the bell housing of the right case half. If in any doubt take the case to an air-cooled Volkswagen specialist.

The other possible cause for concern could be the main bearing seats. If, on examination, you find ridges, particularly in the centre of where the main bearing shells sit in the case, then the case will need to be align-bored (line-bored) by a specialist. Again, if in doubt, show it to a specialist.

The thread holding the cylinder head studs can also fail, resulting in the head becoming loose. This can sometimes be detected by the engine producing a chuffing noise when running. The thread can be repaired by having steel inserts known as case-savers fitted by a specialist. From 1971 these were fitted to all engines at the factory.

CRANKSHAFT

The main and big-end bearing journals should be free of any scratches or overheating damage and be perfectly round, with a mirror finish. The journals should be checked all around using a micrometer, and the maximum out-of-round should not exceed 0.03mm at any point on the journal. If the ovality exceeds this value, the crankshaft will need regrinding by a specialist. Main bearing and big-end shells are available in over and under sizes to suit line-bored cases and reground crankshafts.

CAMSHAFT

Check the cam lobes and bearing journals for wear, and, if in doubt, replace. The cam lobes are

EXAMINATION OF THE ENGINE COMPONENTS

case-hardened and if the thin hardened surface wears away the lobes deteriorate rapidly. So, for a long service life of the engine rebuild, replace the camshaft. Always replace the camshaft bearing shells. This does not apply to 25 and 30PS engines, however, as the camshaft runs directly in the crankcase.

PISTONS AND CYLINDER BARRELS

If you intend to reuse the pistons and barrels, examine the pistons for damage caused by overheating, such as cracks and damage to the rim of the crown. The barrels tend to develop a glaze with use and can benefit from being honed by a specialist.

Fig 6.1 Cylinder barrels being honed to remove the glaze.

CAM FOLLOWERS (TAPPETS)

The surface that contacts the cam lobes tends to become dished with time, so, if in doubt, replace with new, using genuine VW if available. If not, replace with the best quality available; seek advice.

PUSHROD TUBES

These tend to rust and, when reused, spoil the effect of a rebuilt engine.

However, unless you can find new old-stock, genuine VW tubes, it is recommended to treat the rust, expand the concertina ends and reuse the tubes you took off. Recently, the quality of aftermarket pushrod tubes has been very poor. An acceptable alternative, although expensive, is to use the aftermarket spring-loaded type of pushrod tube.

OIL PUMP

Check for wear – your oil pressure depends on it. The pump body and cover tend to become grooved where the gears are spinning against them. However, the cover, if only lightly grooved, can be renovated by using valve grinding paste on a sheet of glass. The technique involves using a figure-of-eight motion to grind away the scratches. Also, the key on the driving gear that slots into the camshaft wears on the corners. If in any doubt, replace the pump. Place a straight edge across the pump body with the gears in place and measure the gap using feeler gauges between the straight edge and the gears. The gap should not exceed 0.004in or 0.1mm, as this may result in poor oil pressure.

CYLINDER HEADS

After removing the valves, clean off all the carbon deposits from the combustion chambers. When clean, check for cracks. This has been a common problem on the later engines, 44PS and larger. Cracks can occur between the valves or between the spark plug and valve. If the cylinder head has come loose, the mating surface between the head and the cylinder barrel may have become burned and pitted. This can be overcome by having the mating surface of the head fly-cut to produce a smooth surface. A spacer shim is then fitted between the head and barrel.

Fig 6.2 *A reamer tool inserted into the valve guide is used to reface the valve seat.*

Fig 6.3 *A valve being re-profiled on a grinding wheel.*

If the valves are tight in the guides when attempting to remove them, it could be due to a carbon deposit on the valve stem, possibly indicating worn piston rings, cylinder bores or valve guides. To check for valve guide wear, push a new valve through the guide until your finger is against the valve guide. Wriggle the valve in each direction until you find where the most play occurs. A new valve should move about 0.25mm at the valve head and a maximum of 0.80mm when worn. If the guides are worn and the cylinder head is in otherwise good condition it may be worthwhile to replace them. In this case, replace all the valves.

The inlet valves are usually reusable after de-coking and lapping in. However, replace the exhaust valves, as reusing them beyond a service life of 60,000 miles isn't worth the risk. A dropped exhaust valve, where the head breaks off the valve stem, causes considerable damage, such as a holed piston and a seized engine. At the very least, this scenario would necessitate the replacement of the piston and barrel set and the cylinder heads, with only the crankcase and its components reusable.

Examine the valve seats and, if they are badly pitted, it is worth having the seats and the valves re-profiled.

TAPPET ADJUSTING SCREWS

Check for wear on the end that contacts the tip of the valve stem. Use genuine VW tappet screws if available, as some aftermarket screws are too soft and wear quickly, causing noisy tappets.

CLUTCH

Faults are not usually apparent until the clutch fails, so unless the unit has been replaced recently it is a good idea to install a new one after an engine rebuild. For a long service life, always replace the clutch as a complete kit, comprising the pressure plate, clutch friction disc and thrust bearing.

CHAPTER 7

ASSEMBLING THE CRANKSHAFT

Tools required:
- Molybdenum or graphite assembly grease or oil
- Hammer and punch
- Torque wrench
- Socket set (13mm for big-end nuts on most engines)
- Locally made tool to hold the crankshaft vertically in a vice. This is made by welding a flywheel-retaining bolt to a short length of square tubing
- Length of 50mm tube, and hammer for tapping home the crankshaft gears
- Camping stove and old saucepan for heating the gears (don't use your partner's best saucepan!)

New parts required:
- Main bearing shells to match the diameter of the bearing journals. These can be supplied under-size in 0.25mm, 0.50mm and 0.75mm and to match the internal bore of the crankcase, over-size in the same increments
- Big-end bearing shells to match the bearing journal diameter, again in the same increments as above

PREPARATION (FIGS 7.1–7.4)

1. If the crankshaft has been reground, use an airline to blow through the oil ways to remove any swarf.
2. Mount the new or reground crankshaft vertically in a vice using a locally produced tool to hold it in place. Alternatively, fit the flywheel locating dowels into the end of the crankshaft, lubricate the no. 1 main-bearing journal, then slip the large circular main bearing onto the crankshaft with the dowel hole nearest the

Fig 7.1 Fit the flywheel-locating dowels into the holes in the end of the crankshaft. The pliers are shown for picture clarity.

Fig 7.2 Lubricate no. 1 main-bearing journal and fit the large circular bearing onto the crankshaft with the locating dowel hole nearest the flywheel.

ASSEMBLING THE CRANKSHAFT

Fig 7.3 Slip two of the three crankshaft end-float shims onto the crankshaft.

Fig 7.4 Fit the flywheel onto the dowels and torque the retaining nut to 80lb ft (110Nm) only. Fit the angle-iron bar to the flywheel, using two of the clutch bolts, to hold the flywheel while tightening the nut. **Refer** to Chapter 5. The crankshaft is shown held in a portable workbench, for illustration only.

flywheel, followed by two of the crankshaft end-float shims, followed in turn by a flywheel to crankshaft gasket (early models only), the flywheel and flywheel gland nut.

Tighten the nut to 80lb ft (110Nm) only, as it will need to be removed before the assembly is fitted to the crankcase. It will be necessary to use the angle iron tool to hold the flywheel while tightening the bolt, or find some other method to prevent it from turning.

3. Using feeler gauges, measure the gap between the flange of no. 1 main bearing and the two shims, subtract 0.1mm (0.004in), and note the difference, as this determines the thickness of the third shim.

4. With the flywheel attached, the assembly can be placed on a bench with the crankshaft vertical ready to receive the rest of the components.

FITTING THE COMPONENTS (FIGS 7.5–7.18)

5. Fit the larger of the two Woodruff keys into the keyway on the crankshaft.

MAIN BEARINGS

- No. 1 is the large flanged circular bearing and is fitted at the flywheel end.
- No. 2 is the split bearing that is fitted in the central position of the crankcase halves, prior to final assembly.
- No. 3 is the other large circular bearing, is flangeless and is fitted between no. 4 connecting rod and the camshaft gear.
- No. 4 is the small circular bearing and is fitted at the pulley end of the crankshaft.

All the bearing shells have holes for locating on the dowels fitted in the crankcase. The holes are not central on the shells and must be fitted with the hole towards the flywheel.

ASSEMBLING THE CRANKSHAFT

Fig 7.5 Place the assembly on a flat surface with the crankshaft vertical and fit the larger of the two Woodruff keys into its keyway.

Fig 7.6 Lubricate no. 3 main-bearing journal and fit the circular main bearing onto the crankshaft with the dowel hole towards the flywheel.

6. Lubricate no. 3 bearing journal. You can use oil, but molybdenum or graphite grease gives more protection at the start-up, before the oil is pushed around the engine by the oil pump. Fit no. 3 circular main bearing shell, remembering to position the dowel hole towards the flywheel.
7. Place the distributor drive gear and the camshaft gear in a pan of boiling water and leave for around five minutes. Place the brass distributor drive gear under the camshaft gear in the water and ensure that the two timing dots on the camshaft gear are uppermost.

   Hook the camshaft gear out of the boiling water and, working quickly, slip the gear onto the crankshaft, align the slot in the gear with the Woodruff key and tap the gear fully home on the shaft using a suitable tubular drift. (Fig 7.7)
8. Fit the spacer, followed by the brass distributor drive gear, using the same procedure as for the cam gear. (Figs. 7.8 and 7.9)
9. Using special circlip pliers with flattened ends, fit the gear-retaining circlip. Ensure that the circlip fits snugly into the groove.
10. Lubricate the small, circular no. 4 main bearing and slide it onto the crankshaft with the dowel locating hole towards the flywheel.
11. Fit the oil deflector disc onto the crankshaft with the concave side towards the crankshaft pulley.

SAFETY

Boiling water creates the potential danger of scalding. Use a tool to remove the hot gears from the boiling water and use heatproof welding gloves to manoeuvre them onto the crankshaft.

ABOVE: Fig 7.8 Slide the spacer onto the crankshaft.

TOP LEFT: Fig 7.7 Place the gears in a saucepan of water and boil for around 15 minutes. Working quickly, take the camshaft gear out of the water and slide it onto the crankshaft with the timing marks up towards the pulley end, and aligned with the Woodruff key. Tap it into position using a length of clean steel tube.

Fig 7.9 Fit the brass distributor drive gear using the same technique as for the camshaft drive gear.

ASSEMBLING THE CRANKSHAFT

ABOVE: *Fig 7.10 Fit the retaining circlip, making sure it fits positively into the groove.*

TOP RIGHT: *Fig 7.11 Lubricate no. 4 bearing journal and slip the circular bearing onto the crankshaft with the dowel hole towards the flywheel.*

Fig 7.12 Fit the oil deflector disc with the concave side towards the pulley.

Fig 7.13 Tap the smaller Woodruff key into the keyway on the end of the crankshaft.

12. Tap the smaller Woodruff key for the crankshaft pulley into the keyway.
13. If the connecting rods have been replaced or had new small-end bearings fitted, check that the piston gudgeon pins slide freely through the small-end bearings.
14. Fit the big-end bearing shells into the connecting rod and the end cap after checking that the bearing surface is clean. The shells have a raised notch that fits into a corresponding notch in the rod and end cap. (Fig 7.14)

Fig 7.15 The forge mark on the connecting rod should face upwards.

Fig 7.14 Fit the big-end bearing shells, ensuring that the raised notch fits neatly into the depression in the connecting rod and cap.

15. Position no. 3 big-end journal (the one nearest the flywheel end) to the left. The connecting rods and bearing end caps are matched pairs and are identified by having the same number on each part. Fit the connecting rods for cylinders 3 and 4 with the small end facing to the right, and the rods for cylinders 1 and 2 to the left. In each case the casting mark, in the form of a raised line halfway up the rod, should face towards you (*see* Figs 7.15 and 7.16).

Rods fitted to 25, 30, 34 and some early 40PS engines are fitted using bolts running through the holes in the connecting rods and into a threaded hole in the end cap. All later units had captive studs fitted to the end cap and are secured with a nut. It is important not to mix the two types. It is recommended to replace the bolts or nuts.

ASSEMBLING THE CRANKSHAFT

Fig 7.16 Fitting the connecting rods is easy to get wrong, so arrange the crankshaft with the bearing journal for number 3 cylinder facing left. Fit the connecting rods for cylinders 3 and 4 with the small ends facing right and the rods for cylinders 1 and 2 facing to the left, with the forge marks towards you.

Fig 7.17 The connecting rod and cap come as a matching pair and the numbers should match and be positioned together.

Fig 7.18 Torque the connecting rod nuts to 24lb ft (33Nm). The rod should rotate freely around the crankshaft with no tight spots. Peen the flange of the nut into the groove on the rod.

Lubricate the bearing surfaces and fit the rods to the crankshaft and lightly tighten the bolts or nuts. Finally, tighten the nuts or bolts with a torque wrench set to 24lb ft (33Nm) for the nuts and 36lb ft (49Nm) for the bolts. When tightening the nuts or bolts, tap the shoulders of the rods with a hammer to release any pre-tension and allow the parts to align correctly.

Prior to the 1973 model year the nuts used were designed to be peened to stop them from undoing. These early rods have a flange that should be peened using a small punch into a groove on the connecting rod. The later rods didn't have this notch and were supplied with nuts that didn't need peening. These nuts may be used on the earlier rods.

CHAPTER 8

REBUILDING THE CRANKCASE

Tools required:
- Molybdenum or graphite assembly grease or oil
- Hammer and punch
- Torque wrench
- Socket set
- Locally made tool to hold the crankshaft vertically in a vice. This is made by welding a flywheel retaining bolt to a short length of square tubing. Alternatively, attach the flywheel to the crankshaft with no. 1 main bearing and two of the end-float shims in place and torque the flywheel retaining bolt to 80lb ft (109Nm)

New parts required:
- Complete engine gasket set
- The reconditioned and assembled crankshaft and rods
- Jointing compound
- Camshaft bearing shells (except for 25 and 30PS engines)
- Crankshaft oil seal

Optional parts (depending on the condition of the originals):
- Tappets (cam followers)
- Tappet adjusting screws
- Camshaft
- Oil pump
- Oil-cooler

1. Remove the flywheel from the crankshaft. It will be necessary to fit the angle-iron tool to the clutch bolt holes in the flywheel to help undo the 36mm flywheel bolt.
2. Both halves of the case must be thoroughly cleaned and the oil ways blown through with an airline to remove all traces of metal particles if the case has been machined. All traces of the jointing compound must be removed from the mating surfaces of the case halves, including the indentions at the base of the studs. Do not use a sharp instrument to do this or the case may leak; instead use a suitable solvent.

Fig 8.1 Fit the dowels into the holes in the main-bearing locations, four in the left case half and one in the no. 2 bearing location in the right case half.

Fig 8.2 Press the bearing shells for no. 2 main bearing into each case half. Position the left-hand case-half between the jaws of a portable workbench or between large blocks, with the cylinder head studs down.

REBUILDING THE CRANKCASE

Fig 8.3 Lubricate the cam followers and insert them in each case half.

Fig 8.4 Check that the camshaft bearing locations are clean and fit the bearing shells into each case half.

3. Fit the main-bearing dowels into the bearing journals, remembering that one fits into no. 2 bearing journal in the right-hand case half. Press the split bearing shells for no. 2 main bearing into their journals.
4. Oil the cam followers (tappets) and fit them into the bores in the case halves. Ensure that the cam followers slide freely in their bores.
5. Fit the camshaft bearing shells into the two case halves. However, 25 and 30PS units do not use bearing shells, as the camshaft runs directly in the case.
6. The cam followers in the right-hand case half will need to be held in place with clips – or sometimes a dab of grease under the head is sufficient.

Fig 8.5 Use spring clips to hold the cam followers in the right-hand case half. Alternatively, a dab of grease behind the head of the cam followers inserted in the right-hand case half may hold them in place long enough to join the two halves of the case.

REBUILDING THE CRANKCASE

Fig 8.6 Check that all three crankshaft end-float shims are in place. Grasp the connecting rods for cylinders 1 and 2 and lift the crankshaft into the crankcase. Rotate the circular main bearings until they engage with the dowels.

7. Place the left-hand case half with the head studs between the jaws of a portable work bench or between suitable blocks on a work surface.
8. Fit the third crankshaft end-float shim of the thickness determined earlier to the crankshaft before lifting the shaft into the crankcase.
9. Turn the bearing shells so that the dowel holes will face downwards when the crankshaft is lifted. Grasp the connecting rods of nos 1 and 2 cylinders and carefully lift the crankshaft assembly into the case. Rotate the main bearing shells until all the shells drop onto their dowels.

    Fit camshaft bearing shells into the bearing saddles in each case half.
10. Rotate the crankshaft into a suitable position to mesh the gear wheel on the crankshaft with the gear on the camshaft. It is correct when the single dot on the camshaft gear is between the two dots on the crankshaft gear.
11. Check that the indentations for the sealing rings are clean, and push the rubber sealing rings onto the six case studs.

Fig 8.7 Loosely install the crankshaft pulley. Rotate the crankshaft so the two dots on the camshaft gear are around 45° to the right when viewed from the pulley end. Mesh the single dot on the cam wheel between the two dots on the crankshaft gear and rotate the camshaft into the bearings. Check that they are correctly meshed.

Fig 8.8 Check that the depressions at the base of the six crankcase studs are clean. Do not use anything sharp to clean them as you may make the case leak. Slip the sealing rings over the six crankcase studs and push them into the indentations at the base of the studs.

REBUILDING THE CRANKCASE

Fig 8.9 Apply a thin coating of Permatex gasket sealant to the mating surfaces of each case half. Coat the camshaft plug with sealant and install it in the left-hand case half with the concave side inwards. Gently lower the right-hand case half onto the studs, taking care not to allow the cam followers to drop out.

Fig 8.10 Install the six 17mm nuts and tighten them, working from the centre out, initially to 11lb ft (15Nm). Tighten all the 13mm nuts to the same torque value.

12. After checking that the mating surfaces of the two crankcase halves are scrupulously clean, coat each half with a thin coat of jointing compound, such as Permatex Super 300 Form-A-Gasket sealant.
13. Coat the camshaft end cap with sealing compound and position it in the case with the concave side facing in.
14. Lift the right-hand case half onto the studs, making sure that the cam followers don't drop out of the upper case half and the rods for cylinders 1 and 2 are through their respective holes in the case half. Press the case half into position and fit the larger nuts onto the studs. These can be M10 or M12 and should be tightened gradually to 11lb ft (15Nm), working from the centre outwards.

    Tighten all the 13mm nuts to 11lb ft (15Nm) and then tighten the 13mm nut next to the lower large nut adjacent to no. 1 bearing to its full torque of 14lb ft (20Nm).

    Returning to the large nuts, tighten them first to 20lb ft (26Nm) and then 25lb ft (35Nm), followed by all the smaller 13mm nuts to 14lb ft (20Nm).

Some units produced in 1966 to engine H 0398525 or F 0991727 were produced with 17mm nuts with built-in sealing washers on the centre pair. These should be tightened to 18lb ft (25Nm) only, with the outer four nuts to 25lb ft (35Nm).

Fig 8.11 Tighten the 13mm nut next to the lower front 17mm nut to its full torque value of 14lb ft (20Nm). Tighten the large nuts progressively to 25lb ft (35Nm).

REBUILDING THE CRANKCASE

Fig 8.12 Apply a thin coating of the gasket sealant on the outside of the crankshaft oil seal and press the seal into position.

Fig 8.13 Oil the oil pressure relief piston and insert it and the spring into the bore at the rear of the crankcase. Repeat this step for the oil pressure control valve, if fitted.

Fig 8.14 Fit a new circular gasket ring to the oil pressure relief valve plug and screw it into place. Repeat this step for the oil control valve, if fitted.

Fig 8.15 Replace the oil pump studs that were removed to release the pump from the case during strip-down.

15. Coat the outer edge of the flywheel oil seal with a thin film of jointing compound and press it into the crankcase, using a readily available circular tool and the flywheel gland nut. This can also be achieved using a flat block of wood and a hammer if the tool isn't available.
16. Oil the relief valve piston and slide it into the bore, followed by the spring and valve cap.
    Later engines have two valves, an oil pressure relief valve and an oil pressure control valve. Both are assembled in the same way. Fit a new metal sealing ring to the oil pressure relief valve cap.
17. Replace the two oil-pump studs removed during the strip-down.
    Check that all traces of gasket have been removed from the crankcase and the oil pump body. Fit the narrow-bordered circular gasket over the oil-pump studs. Early engines were fitted with 6mm studs and later models used 8mm studs.
18. Fit the oil pump body into the crankcase with the hole for the drive spindle at the top.
19. Fit the two gears.

REBUILDING THE CRANKCASE

Fig 8.16 Place the narrow oil-pump gasket over the studs.

Fig 8.17 Install the pump body with the hole for the drive gear at the top.

Fig 8.18 Fit the oil pump gears into the pump body.

Fig 8.19 Place the gasket for the oil pump cover over the studs.

REBUILDING THE CRANKCASE

Fig 8.20 Fit the oil pump cover and tighten the 10mm nuts to 7lb ft (10Nm). On later engines with 13mm nuts, tighten to 14lb ft (20Nm).

Fig 8.21 Tilt the crankcase on its side or flywheel down and install the first of the oil strainer gaskets.

Fig 8.22 Fit the oil strainer onto the studs, followed by the second gasket and the oil strainer plate cover. Tighten the 10mm nuts to 5lb ft (7Nm) only.

20. Fit the wider-bordered circular gasket, followed by the oil pump cover plate.
21. On the oil pump, torque 10mm nuts to 7lb ft (10Nm) and 13mm nuts to 14lb ft (20Nm).
22. Tip the crankcase forward onto the bell housing and fit the first of the two gaskets over the studs for the oil strainer plate and cover.
    Fit the oil strainer, the second gasket, and then the oil strainer plate. Make sure you only torque the 10mm cap nuts to 7lb ft (10Nm).
23. Early Type 1 and Type 2 models used a gasket between the crankshaft and the flywheel, while later models used an O-ring in a recess in the flywheel where it fits over the crankshaft. If the flywheel has a groove for an O-ring in the internal bore where it fits onto the crankshaft, don't use a gasket between the crankshaft and the flywheel. Early models used a paper gasket and this is still included in engine rebuild gasket sets. It has been suggested that this was replaced by a metal gasket for later models as it was reported that flywheels became loose when the paper gasket deteriorated.
    Fit the flywheel on to the dowels and screw in the flywheel gland nut.
    Attach the home-made angle iron tool to the flywheel using two clutch bolts.
    Torque the flywheel gland nut to 217lb ft (294Nm). Due to the high torque required, this operation is best carried out with the engine on the ground (see Chapter 5, Removing the Flywheel).

Fig 8.23 Fit the flywheel O-ring into the groove within the recess that fits onto the crankshaft, install the flywheel onto the crankshaft dowels and hand tighten the 36mm gland nut. With the engine unit placed at ground level, attach the angle iron tool onto the flywheel with two of the clutch bolts. Support the end of the angle iron with a wooden block or a free-standing bench vice. Tighten the 36mm bolt to 217lb ft (294Nm).

24. Before fitting the crankshaft pulley, fit the piece of tinware that is positioned between the pulley and the crankcase. It is held in place by two screws and is impossible to fit once the pulley is in place.

    Fit the crankshaft pulley to the rear of the crankshaft and torque the 30mm nut to 33lb ft (45Nm).

25. Offer the clutch driven plate up to the flywheel and use a centring tool to align the spline with the gearbox input shaft. Generic tools are available for this task but, if obtainable, the best solution is to use a gearbox input shaft. With the centring tool in place, fit the clutch pressure plate using the six bolts removed during strip-down. Gradually tighten the bolts, taking

Fig 8.24 Fit the inner pulley guard onto the rear of the engine with two 6mm-thread screws, either the slotted-head type or 10mm hexagonal head set-screws.

Fig 8.25 Install the crankshaft pulley onto the Woodruff key and tighten the 30mm bolt to 33lb ft (45Nm).

REBUILDING THE CRANKCASE

Fig 8.26 Using a gearbox input shaft or a generic clutch centring tool, offer the clutch driven plate up to the flywheel.

Fig 8.27 Install the clutch pressure plate. Progressively tighten the six pressure-plate bolts and finally fully torque the bolts to 18lb ft (25Nm).

Fig 8.28 Clutch free play measured at the clutch pedal should be between 10 and 20mm.

Fig 8.29 Early models to 1965 used a curved clutch-operating lever. The free play was adjusted using a domed nut that fitted into an indentation in the clutch-operating lever and was held in place with a lock nut.

care to apply pressure evenly to avoid distorting the pressure plate. Torque the bolts to 18lb ft (5Nm).

26. Clutch free play is measured at the top of the pedal and should be between 10 and 20mm. Early models to 1965 are fitted with a curved clutch-operating lever on the left side of the gearbox, and have an adjustment nut with a rounded base that fits into a recess in the operating lever. To adjust the free play, hold the solid threaded adjustment bar with lockable grips, slacken the lock nut and turn the larger nut until the correct free play is achieved. Tighten the lock nut.

Fig 8.30 From 1965 onwards, a straight clutch-operating lever was used and the free play was adjusted using a wing nut.

Fig 8.31 The clutch free play-adjusting wing nut has an elliptical base that fits into a similar indentation in the clutch-operating lever.

Later vehicles are fitted with a straight clutch-operating lever and use a single wing nut to adjust the free play. The wing nut has an elliptical base that fits into a similar recess in the clutch-operating lever. To adjust the free play, clamp the threaded rod at the end of the cable with lockable grips and turn the wing nut half a turn at a time until the correct free play is achieved. Finally, make sure the wing nut clicks into the recess in the operating lever. The wing nut can be very stiff to turn but a round tool is available that fits over the wing nut, making this job easier.

27. Using a long, thin screwdriver or a length of stout wire as a guide, drop the two distributor driveshaft washers down the bore so they seat nicely into position.

With no. 1 cylinder at TDC, oil the distributor driveshaft and guide it into the bore so that the groove that drives the distributor is parallel with the crankshaft pulley and the smaller D section positioned towards the pulley. There is a special tool for this but a suitably whittled piece of wood, such as dowel, works just as well (see Chapter 5, Fig 5.9).

Using the stout wire guide, install the anti-chatter spring into the depression on the top of the distributor drive shaft.

Fig 8.32 Before the distributor driveshaft can be installed, two thrust washers are placed in the crankcase, guided by a screwdriver inserted in the driveshaft locating bore.

Fig 8.33 With no. 1 piston at TDC, lower the distributor driveshaft into the crankcase with the smallest D shape nearest the pulley and the groove that drives the distributor nearly parallel with the pulley. It should be lowered into the hole at around 30° to parallel, as it rotates clockwise as it meshes with the gear. Install the anti-chatter spring into the indentation at the top of the distributor driveshaft.

Fig 8.33A The angle of the distributor driveshaft on 1700, 1800 and 2-litre engines is 12° from the straight to the left of the driveshaft bore. The top of the photograph is towards the flywheel.

On the 1700, 1800 and 2-litre engines, the angle is 12° from the straight edge to the left of the driveshaft bore.

28. Fit a new O-ring around the stem of the distributor and install it into the engine to mesh with the distributor driveshaft. Leave the distributor cap off but install the rotor arm to aid setting up the valve clearances. With no. 1 piston at TDC, turn the distributor body until the groove in the rim of the distributor body is aligned with the centre of the rotor arm. Tighten the bracket onto the stud behind the distributor body on top of the crankcase using a 13mm socket, and tighten the clamp with a 10mm spanner.

29. The valves must be shut at the point of combustion so a small amount of free play in the valve train is required, measured at the tappet adjustment screws in the rocker box.

Refer to Chapter 2 for valve clearance adjustment.

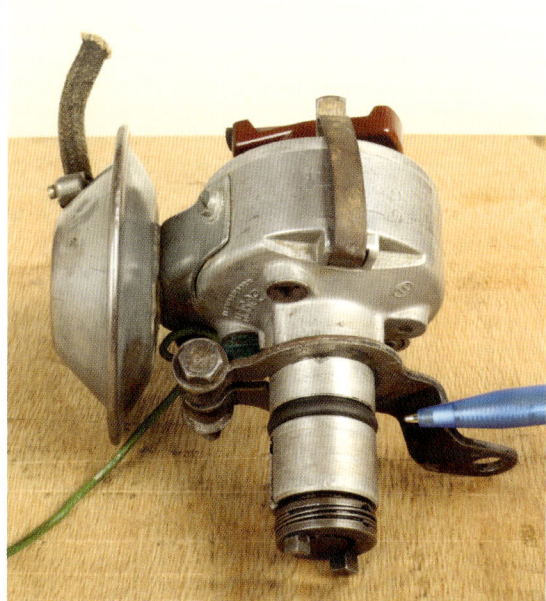

Fig 8.34 Fit a new O-ring around the shaft of the distributor and lower it into the crankcase. Rotate the rotor arm until the shaft meshes with the distributor driveshaft. Check that the rotor arm points towards the indentation on the rim of the distributor body. Tighten the clamp onto the stud on the crankcase.

1700, 1800 AND 2000CC TYPE 4 ENGINES (FIGS 8.35–8.39)

When working on these engines, much the same principles apply as for the Type 1 engine, but there are several detail differences.

REBUILDING THE CRANKCASE

Fig 8.35 Align the fan hub with the Woodruff key in the crankshaft, fit the central bolt and torque to 23lb ft (32Nm).

Fig 8.36 Before fitting the flywheel, check the condition of the gearbox input shaft bearing mounted in the crankshaft. The bearing shown here is new.

The rear of the engine has an oil seal, not the dished oil thrower disc used on the Type 1 engine. The technique for replacing the oil seal is the same as that used when replacing the flywheel oil seal.

To install the fan hub, slide the hub over the Woodruff key in the crankshaft, install the central bolt and tighten it to 23lb ft (32Nm).

If a new gearbox input shaft bearing is needed, it should be inserted into the crankshaft with the felt ring towards the end of the crankshaft; apply grease to the needle roller bearings and a little engine oil on the felt ring on the outer end of the bearing.

The flywheel is mounted on the crankshaft using five bolts and a thin metal plate. Fit a new O-ring into the groove in the nose of the flywheel. Take care not to damage the rolled pin when aligning the flywheel with the crankshaft. Use a new five-holed bolt plate, install the five 17mm headed bolts and torque to 80lb ft (110Nm).

The crankcase halves are held together with through bolts. The six main bearing bolts are 10mm with the bolts around the flanges being 8mm.

Each cylinder head has two rocker shafts, effectively one for each cylinder. Before inserting the pushrod tubes, torque the cylinder-head bolts and install the deflector plate under the cylinders and heads; it is not possible to install the deflector plates

Fig 8.37 Fit a new O-ring oil seal into the groove in the nose of the flywheel. Locate the flywheel onto the rolled pin in the crankshaft, use a new bolt plate, install the five flywheel bolts and torque to 80lb ft (110Nm).

90 REBUILDING THE CRANKCASE

once the pushrod tubes are fitted. Insert the tubes from inside the rocker box. The pushrod tube seals are usually white at the cylinder head and black where the tube enters the crankcase. Smear a little oil on the O-ring and rotate the tube as it is inserted through the rocker box. The pushrod tubes are held in place with a spring clip in the rocker box, and are clipped into place on the underside of the mounting blocks for the rocker shafts.

The exhaust ports face downwards on the cylinder heads, and the mountings for the heat exchangers are bolted up from below and should be fitted with new gaskets. Torque the nuts to 16lb ft (22Nm).

Fig 8.38 The rocker box has separate rocker shafts for each cylinder. Install the deflector plate under the cylinder head and cylinders before inserting the pushrod tubes. The latter are inserted through the rocker box and are held in position by a spring clip. When inserting the pushrod tubes, smear oil on the seals and rotate each tube as it is fitted into place.

Fig 8.39 Cylinder head on the bench with heat exchanger, showing the fixing points on the underside of the head. Always use new gaskets.

CHAPTER 9

REMOVING THE EXHAUST AND ANCILLARIES ON 1700, 1800 AND 2-LITRE TYPE 4 ENGINES

OIL PRESSURE SWITCH (FIG 9.1)

The oil pressure warning light switch is mounted vertically just behind no. 4 cylinder, adjacent to the oil cooler.

OIL-COOLER (FIG 9.2)

The oil-cooler is mounted horizontally on the Type 4 style engine between no. 4 cylinder and the fan housing. Two rubber sealing rings are positioned between the cooler and the engine case and the unit is secured with three fixings.

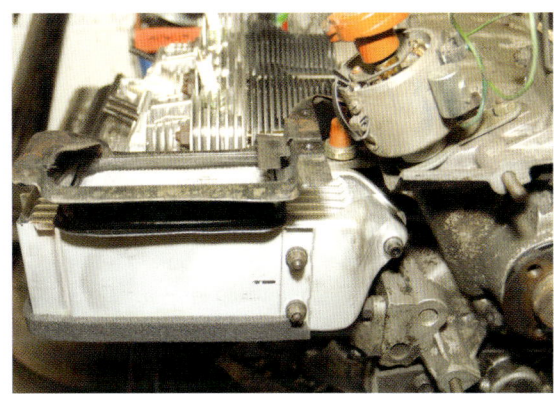

Fig 9.2 The oil-cooler is held by three fixings and is positioned behind no. 4 cylinder. Rubber seals are used between the cooler and the crankcase.

FUEL PUMP (FIG 9.3)

The fuel pump is mounted forward of no. 1 cylinder, close to the flywheel. It is secured with two 6mm Allen bolts.

Fig 9.1 The oil pressure sensor is between no. 4 cylinder and the oil-cooler.

Fig 9.3 The fuel pump is positioned forward of no. 1 cylinder. It is held onto the case with two bolts.

92 REMOVING THE EXHAUST AND ANCILLARIES ON 1700, 1800 AND 2-LITRE TYPE 4 ENGINES

Fig 9.4 A duct forward of the front tinware and next to the fuel pump feeds warm air to the air cleaner.

Fig 9.5 This tube, together with the duct (Fig 9.4), feeds warm air to the air filter.

OIL FILLER PIPE (FIG 9.6)

The oil filler pipe and dipstick tube connection are fitted to the rear of the crankcase near no. 2 cylinder. A gasket is fitted between the case and the oil filler tube and the assembly is secured with two nuts. The dipstick tube passes through the fan housing and is connected with a rubber tube at the base.

AIR INTAKE WARM AIR DUCT (FIGS 9.4 AND 9.5)

At the front of the engine a duct next to the fuel pump collects warm air from under no. 1 cylinder. The duct passes through the front engine tinware and connects to the air cleaner through an adaptor.

COMPLETE FAN HOUSING WITH ALTERNATOR AND FAN (FIGS 9.7, 9.8 AND 9.8A)

The fan housing is secured to the engine case with four 13mm nuts. It can be removed with the

Fig 9.6 The oil filler pipe fits under the fan housing to the rear of no. 2 cylinder. The rubber tube connects to the dipstick tube, which passes through the fan housing.

Fig 9.7 The fan housing complete with alternator fastens to studs on the crankcase with 13mm nuts.

REMOVING THE EXHAUST AND ANCILLARIES ON 1700, 1800 AND 2-LITRE TYPE 4 ENGINES

Fig 9.8 and 9.8A   Remove the plastic cover plate to reveal the alternator belt adjusting screw.

alternator still mounted within after the fan and drive belt have been removed. To remove or adjust the belt tension, remove the cover on the right-hand end of the fan casing. After releasing the pivot bolt at the bottom of the fan housing, slacken or tighten the belt by undoing the bolt on the sliding adjuster to the right of the alternator.

A dowel pin on the fan hub is used to position the fan and spacer. The fan is secured to the hub with three 13mm-headed bolts.

THERMOSTAT (FIG 9.13)

The thermostat is positioned horizontally beneath cylinders 1 and 2 and is connected to air control flaps with a cable, via a pulley wheel, to control the flow of cooling air. When the thermostat is closed,

Fig 9.10   This spacer is fitted between the hub and the fan.

Fig 9.11   The fan is located with a dowel projecting from the hub and is secured with three 13mm bolts.

Fig 9.9   The fan attaches to the hub to the rear of the crankshaft.

Fig 9.12   The fan installed in the fan housing.

94 REMOVING THE EXHAUST AND ANCILLARIES ON 1700, 1800 AND 2-LITRE TYPE 4 ENGINES

Fig 9.13 When adjusting the cooling flaps, check that the operating cable is around the pulley at the right-hand rear of the crankcase.

BELOW: *Fig 9.14 With the engine cold, adjust the flaps so that the right flap is closed and the left flap covers the oil-cooler. The cable adjuster is next to the return spring, close to the right-hand flap. Because the view is from the front of the engine, the left flap in the picture is the right-hand flap when looking from the correct orientation, from the back looking forward.*

the flaps direct air away from the oil-cooler. A spring provides tension to the control cable and, as the thermostat expands, the flaps open to allow cooling air through the oil-cooler. Adjust the flaps when the engine is cold by resisting the spring tension, so that the left flap is covering the oil-cooler. While the left flap is in the lower position, the cooling air avoids the oil-cooler until the engine reaches operating temperature. The adjuster is positioned to the left of the right-hand flap.

CYLINDER COVERS (FIGS 9.17–9.18)

It is important that the cylinder covers and all the additional pieces of tinware that join to them are fitted as intended by the manufacturer, as they control the flow of air around the cylinder heads and cylinder barrels. The rubber seals around the spark plugs should be in good condition for the same reason. The covers fit over tubes from each heat exchanger. Air for the interior heater is blown through the tubes and heat exchanger from an electric fan mounted above the engine.

Fig 9.15 Air from this electric fan, located in the engine compartment, supplies heated air to the car interior.

REMOVING THE EXHAUST AND ANCILLARIES ON 1700, 1800 AND 2-LITRE TYPE 4 ENGINES

Fig 9.16 Air from the electric fan blows air through this tube into the heat exchanger.

Fig 9.17 The left-hand cylinder cover fits over the heater tube and forms a snug fit around the intake ports. It also connects to the front cylinder-head cover.

Fig 9.18 The right-hand cylinder cover also fits around a tube connected to the heat exchanger.

HEAT EXCHANGERS (FIGS 9.16, 9.19 AND 9.20)

The cylinder heads are cross-flow type with the exhaust ports at the bottom when the heads are mounted on the engine. The heat exchangers have two manifold pipes that are connected to the ports, accessed from below the cylinder head. New gaskets should be fitted between the port and the two manifold pipes on the heat exchanger.

Fig 9.19 The heat exchanger connects to the cylinder head with two tubes from below. Gaskets are fitted between the head and the heat exchanger.

96 REMOVING THE EXHAUST AND ANCILLARIES ON 1700, 1800 AND 2-LITRE TYPE 4 ENGINES

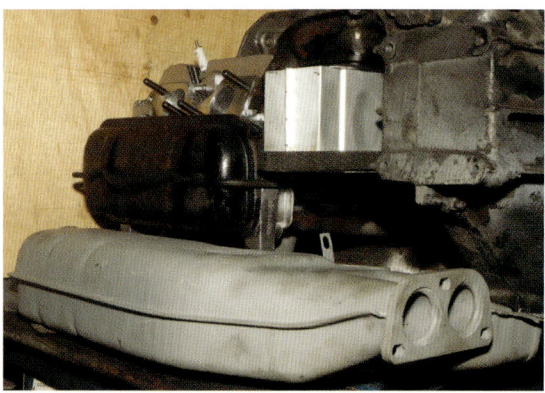

Fig 9.20 The heat exchanger fitted to the engine. The tab on top of the heat exchanger connects to the vertical heater tubes.

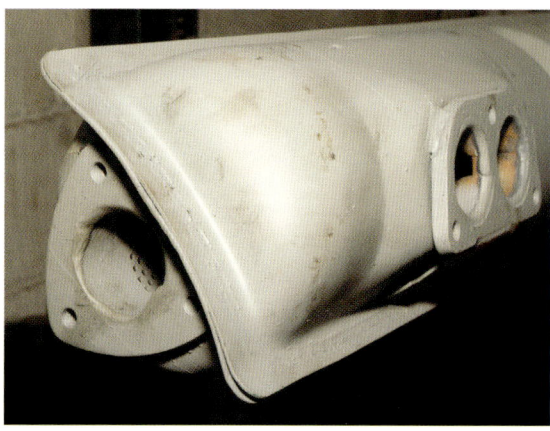

Fig 9.22 The exhaust tailpipe fits to the flange on the end of the exhaust box.

Two types of heat exchanger have been used, the early type having round ports and flanges while the later version has square ports. The two types cannot be interchanged.

Some Type 2 models with later 2-litre engines for the US market have a more complex arrangement, with a separate manifold between the cylinder head and the heat exchanger and other additions. However, in 1979 the heat exchangers bolted directly to the cylinder heads in line with the system used for European markets. California Type 2 models were fitted with catalytic converters.

EXHAUST BOX (FIGS 9.21 AND 9.22)

The exhaust box attaches to the heat exchangers using simple flanges and is held with 13mm bolts. All joints should be fitted with new gaskets.

The exhaust tailpipe is attached to a flange on the end of the exhaust box with three 13mm bolts.

DISTRIBUTOR (FIG 9.23)

The distributor clamp is secured to the crankcase with a 13mm nut forward of the distributor. A screw to the left of the distributor can be loosened to adjust the ignition timing.

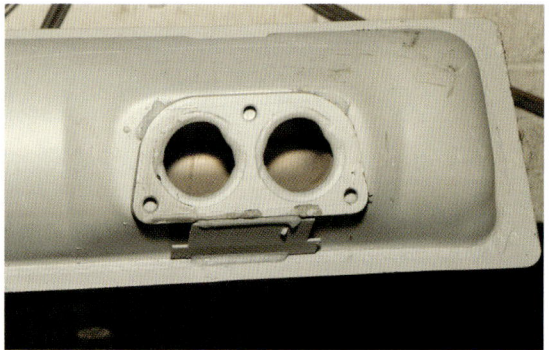

Fig 9.21 The exhaust box showing the flange that connects with the heat exchanger.

Fig 9.23 The distributor adjusting bracket is attached to the crankcase with a 13mm nut forward of the distributor. The bolt to the left of the distributor releases the clamp to adjust the ignition timing.

REMOVING THE EXHAUST AND ANCILLARIES ON 1700, 1800 AND 2-LITRE TYPE 4 ENGINES

Fig 9.24 The scale fitted to the fan housing is used to set the ignition timing.

Fig 9.25 The rear engine mounting brackets illustrated still have the remains of the broken rubber mounts attached.

A scale fitted to the fan housing gives the degrees of ignition advance. The scale is secured with two bolts. Most models are timed using a stroboscopic light at 7.5° before TDC with the vacuum hose disconnected. At maximum revs the total advance should be no more than 32°.

ENGINE MOUNTING BRACKETS (FIGS 9.25 AND 9.26)

The rear engine mounts consist of a sandwich of two metal plates with studs protruding from each plate. The shorter stud is connected to the brackets attached to the engine after the broken mounts shown in Fig 9.25 are removed. The longer studs protrude vertically through the rear engine support bar. The rear engine support bar has substantial brackets at each end that attach to the chassis rails.

Fig 9.26 The outer ends of the rear engine support bar attaches to the chassis rails.

CHAPTER 10

REASSEMBLING THE PISTONS AND CYLINDERS

Tools required:
- Piston ring pliers (ring expander)
- Piston ring clamp
- Long-nosed pliers
- Set of feeler gauges
- A solid, short round bar to use as a drift

If you are reusing the cylinder barrels it may be as well to have them honed by an engineering workshop.

If you are fitting new piston rings, check them in the cylinder bore using feeler gauges. The gap between the ends of the top two compression rings should not be more than 0.90mm and the lower oil scraper ring 0.95mm. If the gaps are excessive it could lead to increased oil consumption and loss of power output due to loss of compression. If you are removing the rings from reused pistons great care needs to be taken, as the rings are easily broken.

Using special piston ring spreader pliers, carefully remove each ring from the piston. Slide each ring in turn about 5mm into the bottom of each barrel using the top of the piston to keep the ring square, and check the gaps using feeler gauges. If all is OK with one set of piston rings you are unlikely to need to check the other pistons. If in any doubt use new pistons and barrels. Refit the rings to the piston using the piston ring pliers. A thin feeler gauge slipped between the ring and the piston opposite the ring pliers helps when slipping the ring over the piston.

Pistons either have an arrow on the crown or on the piston pin housing; when fitted, this should point towards the flywheel.

1. Fit one of the wire piston pin-retaining circlips to no. 1 piston on the side to be nearest the flywheel. The arrow on the crown or under the piston points towards the flywheel. Check that the connecting rod is at TDC.
2. Place the piston pins in the freezer for at least 30 minutes.
3. Ideally using a camping stove and an old saucepan, place each piston in turn into a pan of boiling water. Wear leather welding gloves to protect against scalding. Make sure you know which way the arrow is pointing as it needs to be towards the flywheel when fitted.

Fig 10.1 Fit one of the piston pin wire-retaining clips into each piston.

REASSEMBLING THE PISTONS AND CYLINDERS

4. Remove each piston pin in turn from the freezer and place it close to the work area. Remove the piston from the boiling water and, working quickly, align the hole in the piston with the small-end bearing and slide the piston pin through the piston. You may need to tap it into place using a suitable drift. Retain the piston pin in place using the second wire retaining clip.

   Taking care not to catch the skirt of the piston on the crankcase, rotate the crankshaft to present the next rod to receive its piston and repeat the above procedure for the remaining three pistons.

5. Check the rim of the cylinder bores and remove any remaining traces of gasket. Fit a circular paper gasket to the base of no. 1 cylinder barrel, clamp the piston rings with a piston ring clamp and slide the cylinder barrel onto the studs and over the piston rings.

   When the piston rings are covered by the barrel, remove the piston ring clamp and slide the barrel fully home into the crankcase.

   Fit a short length of pipe over the cylinder stud and secure with a washer and a cylinder head nut. This is to prevent the barrel moving when the crankshaft is turned to fit the no. 2 cylinder barrel.

Fig 10.2 Insert the pin in the piston, line up the pin with the small-end bush and tap the pin home using a suitable drift. Fit the second retaining wire circlip.

   Repeat the same process for no. 2 piston and barrel.

6. Fit the lower cooling-air deflection plate. It has indentations in the brackets that clip to the cylinder-head studs. It is essential to do this before the cylinder heads are fitted.

   Repeat the above procedure for cylinders 3 and 4.

Fig 10.3 Fit a paper gasket to the clean base of the cylinder barrel. Clamp the piston rings with a piston ring clamp and carefully slide the barrel onto the cylinder studs and over the piston rings. Remove the clamp and slide the barrel fully into the crankcase.

Fig 10.4 When cylinders 1 and 2 are in place, fit the lower air deflector plate. It is not possible to fit the air deflector once the cylinder head and pushrod tubes are in place.

CHAPTER 11

REBUILDING AND INSTALLING THE CYLINDER HEADS

Tools required:
- Valve lifting tool
- Valve grinding tool
- Valve grinding paste
- Thin flat-bladed screwdriver
- Molybdenum sulphide paste
- Grease

REBUILDING THE CYLINDER HEADS (FIGS 11.1–11.4)

1. Whether reusing the original cylinder heads or new replacements, it is a good idea to (a) lightly grind in the valves; and (b) match each cylinder barrel to the head to achieve a gas-tight seal.

    If using new heads, remove the valves as described in Chapter 5 and bag up each valve and associated parts and label them so they are returned to their original position.
2. Choose a cylinder barrel and mark it and its position on the cylinder head with a felt-tip pen or Tipp-Ex. Dab small quantities of fine valve grinding paste around the top rim of the cylinder barrel and, using a semi-rotating action, grind it against the cylinder head mating surface. Every now and then lift and rotate the barrel around a quarter of a turn to distribute the grinding paste evenly. When the cylinder head has an even, matt finish without any pitting on the mating surface you are ready to move on to the next cylinder position. Finally, clean off any valve grinding paste. Repeat for each cylinder.
3. Next, grind in the valves to the valve seats. Take each valve and coat the seating area with valve grinding paste. There are fancy and expensive valve grinding tools made but the rubber-sucker type is cheap and just as effective.

Fig 11.1 When grinding in valves, lift and turn the valve grinding tool to spread the grinding paste evenly. If the valve seat is pitted, start with coarse paste and finish of with the fine grade.

Fit the tool on the head of the valve and grind the valve using a semi-rotating action. Remember to lift the valve and turn it quarter of a turn every now and then to spread the paste evenly. When there is a matt grey line around the valve and the valve seat without any pits you are ready to go onto the next valve. Clean each valve and valve seat to remove all traces of valve grinding paste.

4. To reassemble, coat the valve stem with molybdenum sulphide paste and push through the valve guide.

   Fit the valve spring with the tightest coils next to the head. Then fit the valve spring retaining collar and compress the spring with the valve lifting tool until the retaining grooves for the split collets are exposed.

   Grease each half of the split collet and, using a blob of grease on the screwdriver to hold each piece in place, carefully fit each half to the grooves in the valve stem with the narrowest end towards the head of the valve. When both halves of the split collets are fitted snugly on the valve stem, release the valve-spring compressor. Repeat for each valve.

INSTALLING THE CYLINDER HEAD (FIGS 11.5–11.10)

1. For Type 1 engines, prepare the pushrod tubes by fitting the gasket rings on them. The 1700, 1800 and 2-litre Type 4 engines use a different arrangement. The seals are O-ring style and the pushrods are installed after the heads are in position. The tubes should be installed by using a twisting motion as they are being pushed home. They are then held in place by a wire clip that presses on the seal in the cylinder head and is in turn held in place by clipping into a groove in the rocker-shaft pedestal.
2. Place the Type 1 cylinder head on the studs and fit the pushrod tubes loosely into position with the seams facing up. Push the cylinder head further onto the studs and check the pushrod tube seals are a snug fit in the bore in the crankcase and the cylinder head.

Fig 11.2 Coat the valve stem with oil, graphite or molybdenum grease and insert the valve through the valve guide.

Fig 11.3 Fit the valve spring then the valve keeper and compress the spring until the grooves are exposed. Carefully insert the split collets, using a small quantity of grease to hold them in place.

Fig 11.4 When the spring compressor is removed the collets should be neatly held together by the valve keeper.

REBUILDING AND INSTALLING THE CYLINDER HEADS

3. Install all the washers and nuts onto the studs and gradually tighten the nuts using the tightening sequence in Fig 11.6 to a torque value of 7lb ft (10Nm). Then, using the tightening sequence in Fig 11.7, torque the nuts in stages to a final value of 23lb ft (32Nm). Use the latter sequence for both stages when working on 1700, 1800 and 2-litre Type 4 engines; the first stage is to tighten to 11lb ft (15Nm) and the second stage to 23lb ft (32Nm).
4. Install the pushrods. These have been stored so they can be fitted in their original positions, though it probably doesn't matter if new cam followers have been installed.

TOP: Fig 11.5 When fitting Type 1 pushrod tubes, ensure that the seals are sitting squarely in their bores.

MIDDLE: Fig 11.6 For the first stage when tightening the cylinder head nuts on Type 1 engines, use this sequence to a torque of 7lb ft (10Nm).

BOTTOM: Fig 11.7 For Type 1 engines, use this second-stage cylinder head-tightening sequence in stages up to a torque value of 23lb ft (32Nm).

REBUILDING AND INSTALLING THE CYLINDER HEADS

Fig 11.8 Fit sealing rings over the rocker shaft studs.

Fig 11.10 On Type 1 engines, the slots in the rocker arm shaft supports face upwards; on 1700, 1800 and 2-litre engines they face down.

5. Fit new O-ring seals to the rocker arm studs. These have changed over the years so install the same sort from the gasket set that you took off during the strip-down.
6. Install the rocker shaft, taking care to align the cups in the rockers with the pushrods. Torque the 13mm nuts to 18lb ft (25Nm). If the rocker shafts have been dismantled for cleaning, make sure that the slots in the shaft carriers face up.

   Note that 1700, 1800 and 2-litre Type 4 units have two rocker shafts per cylinder head and the 11mm nuts are tightened to 10lb ft (14Nm). Make sure that the pushrods fit snugly into the cups on the rocker arms. On these engines, the slots in the rocker arm shaft supports face down and apply pressure to the pushrod tubes wire retaining spring.
7. After the heads have been installed, adjust the valve clearances to 0.006in or 0.015mm unless a sticker on the fan housing says otherwise. Use good-quality valve-adjusting screws. *See* Chapter 2 for valve clearance adjustment.

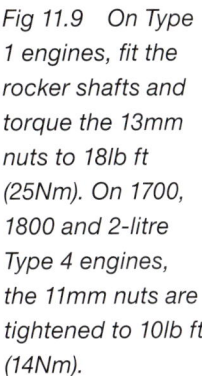

Fig 11.9 On Type 1 engines, fit the rocker shafts and torque the 13mm nuts to 18lb ft (25Nm). On 1700, 1800 and 2-litre Type 4 engines, the 11mm nuts are tightened to 10lb ft (14Nm).

CHAPTER 12

REPLACING ANCILLARIES AND EXHAUST ON TYPE 1 ENGINES

Tools required:
- ⅜in or ½in drive socket set or ring spanners, 8 to 22mm
- Pliers
- 5mm and 6mm Allen key sockets

Before replacing all the ancillaries, the tinware that controls the cooling air should be thoroughly cleaned and painted if necessary; if it is very rusty it may need sandblasting and surface treatments before the final coat of paint is applied.

ATTACHING ANCILLARIES
(FIGS 12.1–12.30)

1. Fit the two cylinder shrouds with two tinware screws into each cylinder head.

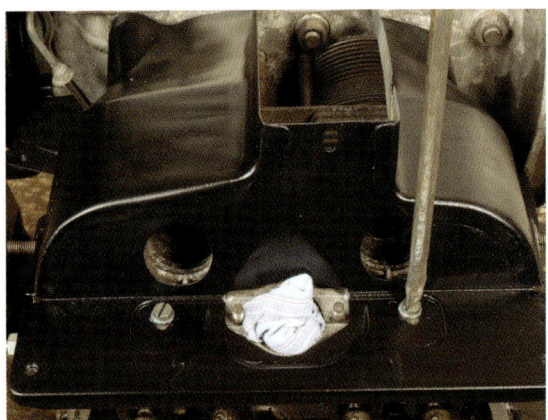

Fig 12.1 Use a flat-bladed screwdriver to attach the cylinder shrouds to the cylinder heads.

Fig 12.2 All single-port engines use a gasket ring between the cylinder head and the inlet manifold.

2. From the gasket set find the rings or gaskets that are positioned before the inlet manifold is attached. Most models use a ring gasket each side between the manifold and the cylinder head.

The exceptions to this are the later 1300cc and 1600cc models that use twin-port cylinder heads. The twin-port-head models were produced from 1971 and have three-part manifolds that are joined with rubber sleeves and clips. As rubber tends to deteriorate over time it is as well to replace them at rebuild time.

On all models except the twin-port units: place the metal sealing rings into the inlet ports in the cylinder heads, offer up the one-piece manifold and tighten the 10mm nuts. Take care not to strip the threads – they only need 7lb ft (10Nm) of torque.

REPLACING ANCILLARIES AND EXHAUST ON TYPE 1 ENGINES

Fig 12.3 Fit the single manifold over the studs on the cylinder head and tighten the nuts to 7lb ft (10Nm) only. You will need to judge this as it is difficult to use a socket.

Fig 12.4 Inlet manifold gaskets for twin-port-head engines are shown at the top, along with the exhaust gaskets and fittings.

For the twin-port engine, loosely connect the three manifold sections before placing the flat metal gaskets over the studs on the cylinder heads.

Offer up the manifold to the head and manoeuvre the two outer sections over the head studs. This can be a bit fiddly as the head studs are positioned at an angle. Add the 13mm nuts and tighten the assembly to the cylinder head.

Finally, manoeuvre the rubber joining pieces to give a nice fit and tighten the clips.

3. Find the rubber seals for the oil-cooler in the gasket set to match the ones you took off. There are several types available, depending on the model year of the engine. In 1970 the diameter of the oil galleries in the engine changed

Fig 12.5 Place the flat metal gaskets over the inlet port studs, followed by the twin-port inlet manifold. Use a ½in AF spanner as it is a better fit on these nuts.

Fig 12.6 The twin-port inlet manifold sections are joined with connectors and held in place with metal clips. The plastic clip attached to the fan housing should hold the spark plug leads in the outer positions with the fuel pipe in the centre.

REPLACING ANCILLARIES AND EXHAUST ON TYPE 1 ENGINES

Fig 12.7 The selection of oil-cooler seals shown here is found in the gasket set. The straight black seals in the foreground fit most single-port engines. Best advice is to replace seals with the same type removed during strip-down. Later engines with a dog-leg oil-cooler, mounted on an intermediate flange, use four seals.

from 8mm to 10mm and the oil-coolers were also made to match the larger size of oil-way. Adaptor seals were made that allow the cooler with the 10mm oil-way to be fitted to the earlier engine. The engines that use a dog-leg cooler forward of the fan housing have an intermediate bracket, necessitating the use of four seals; sometimes just straight tubes and sometimes a stepped seal between the oil-cooler and the crankcase. The best advice is to use the same type of seal that you took off at strip-down.

4. Place the seals in the apertures on the crankcase, then position the oil-cooler on the stud on the top of the crankcase. The two studs protruding from the cooler pass through a flange on the left-hand case half. Tighten the nuts gradually, taking care not to tip the cooler, causing the seals to distort and possibly block the oil-way.
5. On twin-port models, first fit the intermediate flange with two seals between the engine case and the flange. Add two more seals between the flange and the oil-cooler and tighten the nuts evenly to prevent distorting the seals. Alternatively, fit the two parts together before bolting the whole unit to the crankcase.

Fig 12.8 The oil-cooler (or oil-cooler with intermediate flange) is mounted on the crankcase with three 10mm nuts, one on top of the crankcase and two beneath the integral bracket above the cylinders.

Fig 12.9 Fit a gasket above and below the oil deflector plate and make sure that the louvres face downwards, as shown here.

Fig 12.10 Fit the generator or alternator support over the studs and tighten the 13mm nuts to 14lb ft (20Nm).

Fig 12.11 The photograph shows the fan housing fully assembled, with the air deflection boxes and the bar that links them at the front. On twin-port engines with a dog-leg oil-cooler, the link bar and return spring should be left off until the fan housing is in place.

6. Before fitting the generator support bracket to the crankcase, place a gasket over the studs, followed by the baffle plate, as shown in Fig 12.9, and another gasket.
7. Fit the generator or alternator support bracket to the crankcase and tighten the 13mm nuts to 14lb ft (20Nm).
8. Fit the generator or alternator to the fan housing and tighten the four 10mm set screws.
9. Lift the fan housing assembly over the oil-cooler, taking care not to do any damage. Carefully manoeuvre the rod for the thermostat through the hole in the cylinder head; also make sure the edges are inside the flanges of the cylinder shrouds.
10. Tighten the screws on each side of the fan housing.
11. Slide the generator-retaining strap back to fit around the support bracket and tighten the 13mm nut.

Fig 12.12 Lift the fan housing into position and manoeuvre the thermostat linkage through the gap in the cylinder head. Check that the fan housing sits inside the cylinder shrouds. Fit a 6mm threaded screw at each side.

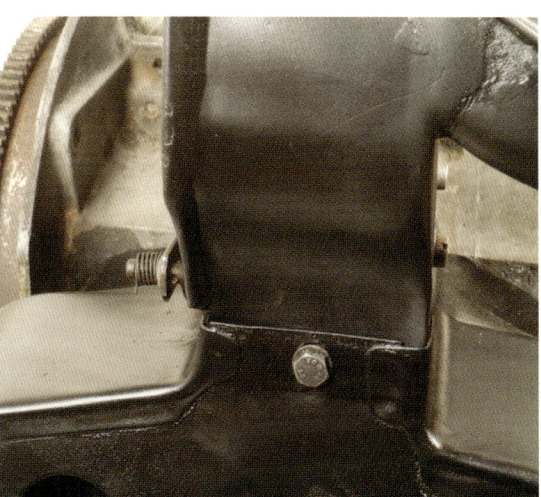

Fig 12.13 Fit and tighten the screws on each side of the fan housing.

Fig 12.14 Slide the generator support strap back to engage with the generator support and tighten the 13mm nut on the support strap.

Fig 12.15 Install the inner pulley half over the keyway on the generator shaft.

12. The inner generator pulley half is located on a keyway on the shaft.

    Add half of the fan-belt adjustment shims to the generator shaft. Wrap the fan belt around the lower pulley, install the outer pulley half and locate it with the lugs into the inner pulley: it will only go on one way. Add the rest of the shims and the domed washer and nut to the shaft. Tighten the nut while allowing the engine to turn; this helps to locate the pulley halves and fan belt. Check the belt tension and refer to Chapter 2 for further adjustment details. The early models located the pulley halves over flats on a hub located on the generator shaft.

13. All models up to July 1964, engine number 8 796 622, have an air regulator ring (throttle ring) fitted to the opening at the front of the fan housing. With the engine warmed up and the thermostat fully open, the top of the ring should be 22mm (0.790in) from the rim of the

Fig 12.16 Wrap the fan belt around the crankshaft pulley; install half of the fan-belt adjustment shims on the generator pulley, followed by the outer pulley half. Add the rest of the adjustment shims, the domed washer and the 21mm nut.

Fig 12.17 The throttle ring was fitted to 25, 30 and 34PS units to engine number 8 796 622 (July 1964). It is fitted with two bolts to the spring-loaded bracket forward of the fan housing.

Fig 12.18 Attach the thermostat to the rod from the fan-housing flaps.

fan inlet funnel. To adjust when the engine is cold, remove the bolt at the base of the thermostat. Place a wedge under the thermostat to hold it at the top of the bracket and measure the gap. Release the return spring from the throttle ring bracket and slacken the clamp nut. Adjust the throttle ring gap to 22mm and tighten the clamp. Re-engage the return spring and check the measurement. If the setting is correct, replace the bolt in the base of the thermostat. Check the gap again when the engine is at full operating temperature.

On all models from August 1964, loosely fit the thermostat support bracket to the crankcase, screw the thermostat to the linkage from the fan housing and attach it to the bracket with the 13mm-headed bolt. Close the flaps by pulling the bracket down against the spring tension and tighten the bracket to the crankcase.

14. On all models from August 1964, except those with a dog-leg oil-cooler, fit the connecting bar across the front of the fan housing that links the air control flaps at the base of the fan housing. At each crank of the air control flaps the bar is held on with a spring clip. Hook the return spring into the bar and the hole in the fan housing.

Fig 12.19 Exit tube for dog-leg oil-cooler. Check that the rubber seals are intact and use one 10mm-headed bolt to connect it to the fan housing. Fit the connecting bar between the air control flaps first.

REPLACING ANCILLARIES AND EXHAUST ON TYPE 1 ENGINES

Fig 12.20 The sloping exit panel for dog-leg cooler is fitted to the fan housing with a 10mm bolt. The rubber seals must be in good order to stop cooling air escaping.

Fig 12.21 Fit the narrow-edged fuel pump gasket over the studs.

Fig 12.22 Install the plastic pushrod guide tube and the pushrod.

Fig 12.23 Fit the fuel pump gasket with just a hole for the pushrod.

Models fitted with the dog-leg oil-cooler have an extra compartment on the front of the fan housing. A sloping bolt-on panel and a tube that passes through the front tinware panel provide an exit for the air that passes through the oil-cooler. Before fitting the exit tube, install the connecting bar between the air deflector boxes in the fan housing. Each crank on the control flaps is connected to the bar with spring clips. Fit the return spring between the fan housing and the connecting bar. Fit the exit tube first and check the condition of the rubber seals where it passes through the front panel. Fit the rubber seal on the top of the exit tube.

Check that the rubber seals are intact and fit the sloping air exit panel between the oil-cooler and the exit tube. Both are attached using a single 10mm bolt for each part.

Place the narrow-bordered gasket over the fuel-pump studs, followed by the plastic push-

Fig 12.24 Apply grease to the underside of the fuel pump, install the pump on the studs and tighten the two 13mm nuts.

Fig 12.25 At the rear of the engine, attach the small tinware pieces to the underside of the cylinder shrouds. This example has a hole for the warm-air feed to the carburettor.

rod guide tube, the gasket with a hole for the pushrod and the pushrod itself. At maximum height the pushrod should project 13mm above the pushrod guide tube. If it is more than 13mm, add more gasket material.

Grease the operating lever on the underside of the fuel pump and install it on the studs using a 13mm spanner.

15. Fit the lower engine tinware panels; at the front they are screwed to the underside of the cylinder shrouds. Two screws secure them to the sides of the crankcase and two more screws secure them to the brackets on the heat exchangers. The right-hand lower tinware panel is in two sections, with the rear section removable to allow access to the thermostat. At the rear of the engine two small tinware panels are attached to the underside of the cylinder shrouds.
16. Check that the control levers on the heat exchangers are not seized. Install metal gaskets on the front exhaust-port studs, fit the heat exchanger and tighten the two 13mm nuts. Access to these nuts can be tedious, so using a C- or S-shaped spanner is recommended. The two brackets on the side of the heat exchangers must be below the lower cylinder tinware panel and fastened to it with two 6mm threaded screws.

Fig 12.26 Install a metal gasket on the front exhaust ports and install the heat exchangers. Check that the two brackets attached to the heat exchangers are under the lower tinware panel and fasten with two 6mm threaded screws.

Fig 12.27 Prepare the engine to receive the exhaust box; fit gaskets on the rear exhaust ports, and the sealing ring and metal retaining ring on the heat exchanger pipes.

112 REPLACING ANCILLARIES AND EXHAUST ON TYPE 1 ENGINES

Fig 12.28 Measure the depth of the tailpipe stubs on the exhaust box. Transfer the measurement to the tailpipes and mark with a fine-tip marker.

Fig 12.29 Push the sealing ring and metal retaining ring to the mark on the tailpipe and install each tailpipe into the exhaust box.

17. Prepare to fit the exhaust box by installing the metal ring and heatproof sealing ring on the rear of the heat exchanger pipe and metal gaskets on the rear cylinder-head exhaust ports.
18. Prepare the exhaust box by pre-fitting the tailpipes. Measure the tailpipe stubs on the exhaust box. Transfer this measurement to the tailpipe and make a small pen mark, slide the sealing ring and metal retaining ring to this mark and install the tailpipe into the stubs on the exhaust box.
19. Fit and tighten the clamps.
20. Fit the exhaust box to the engine, ensuring that the heat exchanger pipes enter the lower exhaust-box pipes and that the gaskets are on the upper studs. Fit a nut to each side on the upper exhaust ports but don't fully tighten until the hotspot connections are lined up. Install the gaskets between the hotspot pipe and the flange at the top of the exhaust box and then use a small crosshead screwdriver to manipulate the hotspot pipe into position so

Fig 12.30 Fit the clamp and tighten the nuts and bolts.

REPLACING ANCILLARIES AND EXHAUST ON TYPE 1 ENGINES

that the first 10mm bolt can be installed. Repeat for the other side, and, when all the hotspot connections are fitted, the nuts on the upper exhaust-box flange can be tightened. Fit and tighten the clamps around the heat exchanger pipes.

The hotspot pipe gaskets have two aperture sizes; one of each should be fitted, as this encourages the hot exhaust gases to flow to heat the inlet manifold. Some later models are fitted with twin hotspot pipes, and these require a special two-holed gasket.

Pods surrounding the upper pipes on the exhaust box connect to the heat exchanger with a wide clamp. Two short metal tubes fit into the top of the pod and these are connected to the fan housing with cardboard tubes after the engine and rear tinware tray is installed. The pods and where the metal tubes pass through the rear tinware panel are often a poor fit.

Fig 12.31 The engine ready to be installed; note the carburettor is not fitted at this stage. It's also a good idea to remove the plug caps and tuck the leads out of the way.

INSTALLING THE ENGINE (FIGS 12.32–12.34)

Installation of the engine is essentially the reverse of the removal procedure. Refer to all the safety procedures described in Chapter 3.

The carburettor is fitted after the engine is installed to prevent it from getting damaged. Likewise, it is advisable to remove the plug cap and leads and tuck them out of harm's way.

21. Lift the engine with the trolley jack, taking care not to damage the clutch or the gearbox input shaft. Lift until the lower engine studs align with the holes in the gearbox bell housing. Before going any further, feed the accelerator cable into the guide tube. Lift and push the engine forward until the clutch-driven plate engages with the splines on the gearbox input shaft. Continue pushing until the engine is fully home against the gearbox.

22. From below, place the nuts on the lower engine studs, then, on later models with a captive nut at the top left of the crankcase, fit the bolt from under the vehicle. Attach the fuel pipe, the heater cables and the plastic tubes that join the heat exchangers to the heater channels. Check that the top right bolt is pushed through to

Fig 12.32 Fit the carburettor to the manifold and tighten the nuts using a C- or S-shaped spanner on the difficult-to-reach forward nut.

the engine bay. On early models the top bolts needed an assistant to hold the top engine bolt with a spanner while the nuts forward of the fan housing are tightened. During the 1960s the top bolt had a D-shaped head to prevent it from turning. Tighten the engine securing bolts to 22lb ft (30Nm).

23. Before fitting the rear engine tinware tray, check that the rubber engine seal is fitted correctly. On early models one half of the seal should be below the side and rear tinware and the other half above. Later models had a J-shaped seal that should be tucked in below the tinware.

24. Fit a new gasket on the inlet manifold and install the carburettor. Use a C-shaped spanner on the nut forward of the carburettor. Connect the accelerator cable and check that the throttle opens to within 1mm of the stop and that it closes fully when the pedal is released. On early models the accelerator return spring surrounded the cable and was covered by a sleeve that tucked in behind the thickened cable end. On later models the return spring is mounted on the carburettor. Connect the choke cable on 25 and 30PS engines.

On all carburettors up to 30 PICT 2 the idle speed is adjusted with the screw at the end of the throttle lever, and the mixture is controlled with the small screw on the left of the carburettor. For 30 PICT 3 and later carburettors, the idle speed was controlled by the larger screw on the left of the carburettor body. The screw on the throttle was factory set and should not be adjusted, though this advice has been largely ignored over the years.

25. Fit the air filter and connect any warm air pipes to the connectors on the engine. Thread the warm air pipes, if fitted, through the rear tinware tray and install the tray to the engine compartment. Tighten all the tinware screws and fit the pulley guard.

Fig 12.33 Fasten the accelerator cable to the connector and adjust the cable to give full throttle without straining the cable.

Fig 12.34 Connect the choke cable (25 and 30PS engines only).

CHAPTER 13

REPLACING ANCILLARIES ON 1700, 1800 AND 2-LITRE TYPE 4 ENGINES

The oil-cooler is horizontally mounted on the left rear of the crankcase behind no. 4 cylinder.

1. Fit the oil seals between the cooler and the crankcase and evenly tighten the three nuts to 5lb ft (7Nm) only. The black surround on the top of the oil-cooler just slides down in front of the oil-cooler and is attached to the tinware at a later stage.

The air control flaps are closed when the engine is cold. When the horizontally mounted thermostat expands, the control flap return spring takes up the slack in the cable, opening the flap to allow the cooling air to pass through the oil cooler.

The thermostat cable passes over a pulley mounted at the lower right-hand rear of the crankcase. The cable then travels vertically to the cooling flap adjuster to the left of the right-hand flap.

A duct mounted to the right front of the engine harvests warm air from under no. 1 cylinder. This is connected to another duct that passes through the front tinware panel and

Fig 13.1 The horizontally attached oil-cooler.

REPLACING ANCILLARIES ON 1700, 1800 AND 2-LITRE TYPE 4 ENGINES

Fig 13.2 The air-control flaps restrict the airflow to the oil-cooler during engine warm-up.

BELOW: Fig 13.3 When the flaps are raised by the thermostat, more air is available to flow over the cylinders, cylinder heads and the oil-cooler.

ABOVE: Fig 13.4 The pulley shown is for the cable that runs between the thermostat and the air-control flaps.

RIGHT: Fig 13.5 The duct on the front of the engine supplies warm air from under no. 1 cylinder to the air-cleaner during warm-up.

REPLACING ANCILLARIES ON 1700, 1800 AND 2-LITRE TYPE 4 ENGINES

Fig 13.6 This duct is in the engine compartment and connects to the duct shown in Fig 13.5.

Fig 13.7 Fit a new gasket to the oil breather. A spring clip holds it in place.

connects to the air filter to supply warm air to the carburettors or fuel injection system.

2. Fit a new gasket and refit the oil breather to the top of the crankcase.
3. Refit the bracket for the oil filter with a new gasket installed. Smear a small quantity of oil on the seal of the filter and hand tighten it into position.
4. If the fan housing has been removed to allow work on the engine, there is no need to remove the alternator. To refit, attach the fan housing onto the four studs to the rear of the crankcase. Fit the spacer and the fan onto the locating dowel on the fan hub and tighten the three bolts to 14lb ft (20Nm). To fit and adjust the fan belt, first remove the oblong cover in the alternator guard, loosen the adjuster and fit the fan belt around the fan and the alternator pulleys. Rotate the alternator on the lower pivot bolt to tension the fan belt and tighten the bolt on the adjuster.

Fig 13.8 The fan housing attaches to the rear of the engine with four 13mm nuts.

118 REPLACING ANCILLARIES ON 1700, 1800 AND 2-LITRE TYPE 4 ENGINES

Fig 13.9   The spacer is fitted to the fan hub and is located on the dowel prior to fitting the cooling fan.

Fig 13.10   The underside of the fan showing the hole for the locating dowel.

Fig 13.11   The fan hub.

Fig 13.12   The fan being fitted onto the fan hub.

Fig 13.13   Remove the plastic oblong cover to reveal the adjuster for the fan-belt tension.

Fig 13.14   Rotate the alternator on the lower pivot and tighten the adjuster bolt.

REPLACING ANCILLARIES ON 1700, 1800 AND 2-LITRE TYPE 4 ENGINES

Fig 13.15 Refit the oil filler pipe using a new gasket. Attach the rubber connecter to the dipstick tube.

Fig 13.16 The fuel pump is located forward of no. 1 cylinder.

5. Use a new gasket when fitting the oil filler pipe to the right-hand rear of the crankcase. Attach the rubber connector to the dipstick tube.
6. The fuel pump is mounted near the flywheel forward of no. 1 cylinder. To refit the pump, grease the pushrod and the pump lever with molybdenum grease, use new gaskets each side of the plastic insulating block and tighten the socket head (Allen) screws. Use new rubber hoses and hose clips if in any doubt regarding their condition.
7. Locate the distributor body into the bore in the crankcase. Engage the drive dog into the slot in the distributor driveshaft and tighten the clamp onto the stud on top of the crankcase. Check that the anti-chatter spring is in the indentation in the top of the distributor drive shaft.

Fig 13.17 When fitting the distributor, rotate the rotor arm to engage the drive dog into the slot in the distributor driveshaft.

120 REPLACING ANCILLARIES ON 1700, 1800 AND 2-LITRE TYPE 4 ENGINES

Fig 13.18 Use new gaskets when connecting the heat exchanger to the cylinder head. The exhaust ports are on the underside of the cylinder head.

Fig 13.19 The fan for the vehicle heater is mounted above the engine in the Transporter.

Fig 13.20 Flexible hoses connect the fan motor to tubes attached to the top of the heat exchangers.

Fig 13.21 At the front of the heat exchanger, metal tubes connect to the vehicle interior pipework.

Fig 13.22 The oil pressure sensor is between the oil-cooler and the distributor.

8. The heat exchangers locate onto studs on the underside of the cylinder heads. Fit new gaskets and tighten to 16lb ft (22Nm). *Refer to Fig 9.19 in Chapter 9.*

   Air from a fan mounted above the engine blows air through tubes mounted above the heat exchangers. The warmed air then flows to the vehicle via tubes attached to the front of the engine.

REPLACING ANCILLARIES ON 1700, 1800 AND 2-LITRE TYPE 4 ENGINES

Fig 13.23 The exhaust silencer box attaches to the flanges at the rear of the heat exchangers.

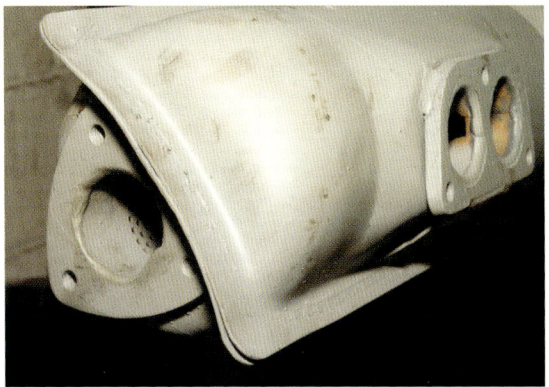

Fig 13.24 A tailpipe attaches to the end of the silencer.

Fig 13.25 The left cylinder cover extends over the oil-cooler.

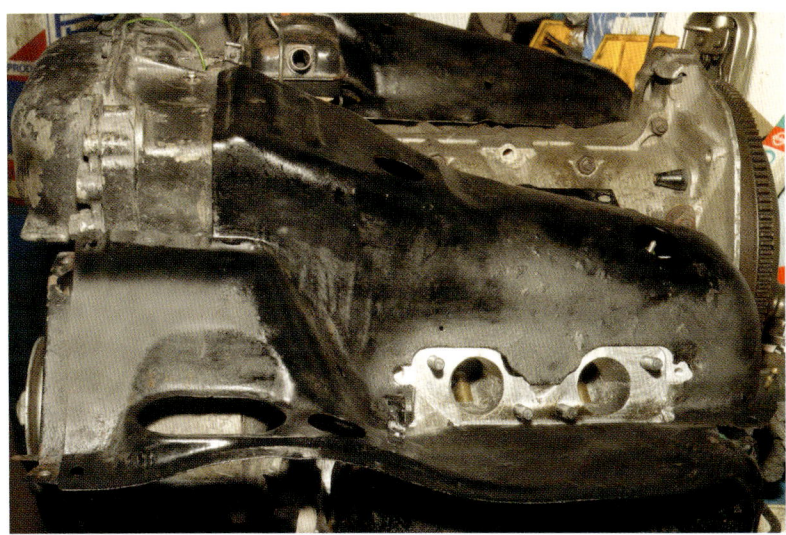

Fig 13.26 The right-hand cylinder cover.

9. Refit the oil pressure sender unit to the left and forward of the distributor.
10. To fit the exhaust box, use two new gaskets between the heat-exchanger flanges and the silencer and tighten the bolts to 14lb ft (20Nm). The tailpipe is attached to the silencer with three 13mm bolts; use a new gasket.
11. Fit the upper cylinder covers and any remaining tinware that attaches to them.
12. On all Transporters from 1968 and on Type 4 models, three 13mm bolts are used at each end to attach the rear engine support bar to the frame. Two brackets are attached to the rear of the engine to hold the rear engine mounts. A plate is bonded to the rubber with a single stud that passes through the engine mount brackets. On the underside of the engine mount is another plate bonded to the rubber engine mount. The studs on the lower plate are longer and pass through the engine support bar. Tighten all the nuts to 14lb ft (120Nm).

Fig 13.27 The rear engine-support bar attaches to the frame at each end with three bolts.

Fig 13.28 The remains of the rear rubber engine mounts can be seen under the brackets. There should be a thick rubber mount with studs pointing down to attach to the engine support bar.

APPENDIX I

SPECIFICATIONS

TYPE 1 25PS ENGINE

Type	4-stroke horizontally opposed air-cooled engine
Cylinders	4
Capacity	1131cc
Bore	75mm
Stroke	64mm
Compression ratio	5.8:1
Cylinders	Individual cast iron, finned for air cooling
Cylinder head	Cast aluminium, finned for air cooling
Crankshaft	Steel forging with four main bearings
Main bearings 1, 3, 4	Circular sleeve bearings
Main bearing 2	Two bearing shells
Big-end bearings	Lead bronze alloy, steel-backed
Small-end bearings	Pressed-in bronze bushes
Pistons	Steel-reinforced aluminium alloy
Piston rings	Two compression and one oil control ring
Camshaft	Grey cast with three bearings machined in the case
Camshaft drive	Helical gears from the crankshaft
Valves	Overhead
Valve clearances	0.006in or 0.015mm
Cooling	Fan, driven by V-belt from crankshaft
Oil cooling	Oil-cooler in airstream from the fan
Static ignition timing	5° before TDC
Firing order	1–4–3–2
Ignition advance	Centrifugal mechanism
Contact breaker gap	0.016in or 0.40mm
Carburettor	Solex 26VFIS, downdraught type

TYPE 1 30PS ENGINE

Type	4-stroke horizontally opposed air-cooled engine
Cylinders	4
Capacity	1192cc
Bore	77mm
Stroke	64mm
Compression ratio	6.1:1 up to July 1955; 6.6:1 from August 1955
Cylinders	Individual cast iron, finned for air cooling
Cylinder head	Cast aluminium, finned for air cooling
Crankshaft	Steel forging with four main bearings
Main bearings 1, 3, 4	Circular sleeve bearings
Main bearing 2	Two bearing shells
Big-end bearings	Lead bronze alloy, steel-backed
Small-end bearings	Pressed-in bronze bushes
Pistons	Steel-reinforced aluminium alloy
Piston rings	Two compression and one oil control ring
Camshaft	Grey cast with three bearings machined in the case
Camshaft drive	Helical gears from the crankshaft
Valves	Overhead
Valve clearances	0.006in or 0.015mm
Cooling	Fan, driven by V-belt from crankshaft
Oil cooling	Oil-cooler in airstream from the fan
Static ignition timing	7.5° before TDC
Firing order	1–4–3–2
Ignition advance	Centrifugal mechanism and vacuum
Contact breaker gap	0.016in or 0.40mm
Carburettor	Solex 28 PCI, downdraught type with accelerator pump

TYPE 1 34PS ENGINE

Type	4-stroke horizontally opposed air-cooled engine
Cylinders	4
Capacity	1192cc
Bore	77mm
Stroke	64mm
Compression ratio	7:1
Crankcase	Magnesium alloy
Cylinders	Individual cast iron, finned for air cooling
Cylinder head	Cast aluminium, finned for air cooling
Crankshaft	Steel forging with four main bearings
Main bearings 1, 3, 4	Circular sleeve bearings
Main bearing 2	Two bearing shells
Big-end bearings	Lead bronze alloy, steel-backed
Small-end bearings	Pressed-in bronze bushes
Pistons	Steel-reinforced aluminium alloy
Piston rings	Two compression and one oil control ring
Camshaft	Grey cast with three bearings machined in the case up to 1965; grey cast with three bearings running in aluminium shells from 1965
Camshaft drive	Helical gears from the crankshaft
Valves	Overhead
Valve clearances	Inlet 0.008in or 0.20mm, exhaust 0.008 or 0.20mm. From August 1965 or if a sticker on the fan housing indicates 0.004in or 0.10mm set both valves to 0.006in or 0.15mm
Cooling	Fan, driven by V-belt from crankshaft
Oil cooling	Oil-cooler in airstream from the fan
Static ignition timing	10° before TDC up to July 1966; 7.5° from August 1966
Firing order	1–4–3–2
Ignition advance	Centrifugal mechanism and vacuum
Contact breaker gap	0.016in or 0.40mm
Carburettor	Solex 28 PICT or 28 PICT-1, downdraught type

TYPE 1 40PS ENGINE

Type	4-stroke horizontally opposed air-cooled engine
Cylinders	4
Capacity	1285cc
Bore	77mm
Stroke	69mm
Compression ratio	7.3:1
Crankcase	Magnesium alloy
Cylinders	Individual cast iron, finned for air cooling
Cylinder head	Cast aluminium, finned for air cooling
Crankshaft	Steel forging with four main bearings
Main bearings 1, 3, 4	Circular sleeve bearings
Main bearing 2	Two bearing shells
Big-end bearings	Lead bronze alloy, steel-backed
Small-end bearings	Pressed-in bronze bushes
Pistons	Steel-reinforced aluminium alloy
Piston rings	Two compression and one oil control ring
Camshaft	Grey cast with three bearings running in aluminium shells
Camshaft drive	Helical gears from the crankshaft
Valves	Overhead
Valve clearances	0.006in or 0.015mm
Cooling	Fan, driven by V-belt from crankshaft
Oil cooling	Oil-cooler in airstream from the fan
Static ignition timing	7.5° BTDC to engine number F2 140 820
Firing order	1–4–3–2
Ignition advance	Vacuum only advance
Contact breaker gap	0.016in or 0.40mm
Carburettor	Solex 30 PICT-1 or 30 PICT-2, downdraught type

TYPE 1 44PS ENGINE

Type	4-stroke horizontally opposed air-cooled engine
Cylinders	4
Capacity	1493cc
Bore	83mm
Stroke	69mm
Compression ratio	7. 5:1
Crankcase	Magnesium alloy
Cylinders	Individual cast iron, finned for air cooling
Cylinder head	Cast aluminium, finned for air cooling
Crankshaft	Steel forging with four main bearings
Main bearings 1, 3, 4	Circular sleeve bearings
Main bearing 2	Two bearing shells
Big-end bearings	Lead bronze alloy, steel-backed
Small-end bearings	Pressed-in bronze bushes
Pistons	Steel-reinforced aluminium alloy
Piston rings	Two compression and one oil control ring
Camshaft	Grey cast with three bearings running in aluminium shells
Camshaft drive	Helical gears from the crankshaft
Valves	Overhead
Valve clearances	Inlet 0.012in or 0.30mm. From August 1965 or a sticker on fan housing indicates 0.004in or 0.10mm set both valves to 0.006in or 0.15mm
Cooling	Fan, driven by V-belt from crankshaft
Oil cooling	Oil-cooler in airstream from the fan
Static ignition timing	a. 7.5° BTDC to engine number H0 879 926
	b. 0° engine numbers H0 879 927 to H1 124 669 (auto stick-shift)
	c. 7.5° BTDC engine number H1 124 670 to H1 259 314
Firing order	1–4–3–2
Ignition advance	a. Vacuum only advance
	b. Centrifugal advance and vacuum advance and retard
	c. Vacuum only advance
Contact breaker gap	0.016in or 0.40mm
Carburettor	Solex 30 PICT-1 or 30 PICT-2, downdraught type

TYPE 1 1300CC 44PS TWIN-PORT ENGINE

Type	4-stroke horizontally opposed air-cooled engine
Cylinders	4
Capacity	1285cc, engine codes AB and AR
Bore	77mm
Stroke	69mm
Compression ratio	7.5:1
Crankcase	Magnesium alloy
Cylinders	Individual cast iron, finned for air cooling
Cylinder head	Twin inlet-port cast aluminium, finned for air cooling
Crankshaft	Steel forging with four main bearings
Crankshaft end-float	0.07 to 0.13mm
Main bearings 1, 3, 4	Circular sleeve bearings
Main bearing 2	Two bearing shells
Big-end bearings	Three-layer shells
Small-end bearings	Pressed-in bronze bushes
Pistons	Steel-reinforced aluminium alloy
Piston rings	Two compression and one oil control ring
Camshaft	Grey cast with three bearings running in aluminium shells
Camshaft drive	Helical gears from the crankshaft
Valves	Overhead
Valve clearances	0.006in or 0.015mm
Cooling	Fan, driven by V-belt from crankshaft
Oil cooling	Oil-cooler in airstream from the fan
Static ignition timing	a. 5° ATDC engine numbers AB0 000 001 to AB0 313 345
	b. 7.5° BTDC engine number AB0 313 346 onwards
Firing order	1–4–3–2
Ignition advance	a. centrifugal advance and vacuum advance and retard
	b. vacuum only advance
Contact breaker gap	0.016in or 0.40mm
Carburettor	Solex 31 PICT-4, downdraught type

TYPE 1 47 AND 50PS ENGINE

Type	4-stroke horizontally opposed air-cooled engine
Cylinders	4
Capacity	1584cc, engine codes AB and AR
Bore	85.5mm
Stroke	69mm
Compression ratio	7.5:1 from April 1968 Transporter, 8:1 Beetle
Crankcase	Magnesium alloy
Cylinders	Individual cast iron, finned for air cooling
Cylinder head	Single inlet port 47PS Transporter to July 1970
	Twin inlet port cast aluminium 50PS from August 1970
Crankshaft	Steel forging with four main bearings
Crankshaft end-float	0.07 to 0.13mm
Main bearings 1, 3, 4	Circular sleeve bearings
Main bearing 2	Two bearing shells
Big-end bearings	Three-layer shells
Small-end bearings	Pressed-in bronze bushes
Pistons	Steel-reinforced aluminium alloy
Piston rings	Two compression and one oil control ring
Camshaft	Grey cast with three bearings running in aluminium shells
Camshaft drive	Helical gears from the crankshaft
Valves	Overhead
Valve clearances	0.006in or 0.015mm
Cooling	Fan, driven by V-belt from crankshaft
Oil cooling	Oil-cooler in airstream from the fan
Static ignition timing	a. 0° TDC B series engine
	b. 5° ATDC AD series to 279 999, AE to 999 999, AK to 120 008, AH to 090 023
	c. 7.5° BTDC AD series from 280 000, AK 120 009 on, AH 090 0244 on
Firing order	1–4–3–2
Ignition advance	a. Centrifugal advance and vacuum advance and retard
	b. Centrifugal advance and vacuum advance and retard
	c. Vacuum advance only
Contact breaker gap	0.016in or 0.40mm
Carburettor	Solex 30 PICT-3 on 47PS, 34 PICT-3 or 34 PICT-4 on 50PS

TYPE 1 54PS ENGINE USED IN TYPE 3

Type	4-stroke horizontally opposed air-cooled engine
Cylinders	4
Capacity	1493cc
Bore	83mm
Stroke	69mm
Compression ratio	7.2:1 to July 1963; 7.8:1 from August 1963
Crankcase	Magnesium alloy
Cylinders	Individual cast iron, finned for air cooling
Cylinder head	Single inlet-port cast aluminium, finned for air cooling
Crankshaft	Steel forging with four main bearings
Crankshaft end-float	0.07 to 0.13mm
Main bearings 1, 3, 4	Circular sleeve bearings
Main bearing 2	Two bearing shells
Big-end bearings	Three-layer shells
Small-end bearings	Pressed-in bronze bushes
Pistons	Steel-reinforced aluminium alloy
Piston rings	Two compression and one oil control ring
Camshaft	Grey cast with three bearings running in aluminium shells
Camshaft drive	Helical gears from the crankshaft
Valves	Overhead
Valve clearances	0.012in or 0.30mm. From August 1965 or if a sticker indicates 0.004in or 0.10mm set both valves to 0.006in or 0.15mm
Cooling	Fan, driven directly from the crankshaft
Oil cooling	Horizontal oil-cooler in airstream from the fan
Static ignition timing	a. 7.5° BTDC 1500N to July 1963
	b. 10° BTDC 1500N, 1500A and 1500S
Ignition advance	Centrifugal and vacuum 1500S August 1963 to July 1964; all others vacuum only
Firing order	1–4–3–2
Contact breaker gap	0.016in or 0.40mm
Carburettor	Single Solex 32 PHN-1, side-draught type

TYPE 1 65PS ENGINE USED IN TYPE 3 1500S

Type	4-stroke horizontally opposed air-cooled engine
Cylinders	4
Capacity	1493cc
Bore	83mm
Stroke	69mm
Compression ratio	8.5:1
Crankcase	Magnesium alloy
Cylinders	Individual cast iron, finned for air cooling
Cylinder head	Single inlet-port cast aluminium, finned for air cooling
Crankshaft	Steel forging with four main bearings
Crankshaft end-float	0.07 to 0.13mm
Main bearings 1, 3, 4	Circular sleeve bearings
Main bearing 2	Two bearing shells
Big-end bearings	Three-layer shells
Small-end bearings	Pressed-in bronze bushes
Pistons	Steel-reinforced aluminium alloy
Piston rings	Two compression and one oil control ring
Camshaft	Grey cast with three bearings running in aluminium shells
Camshaft drive	Helical gears from the crankshaft
Valves	Overhead
Valve clearances	0.012in or 0.30mm. From August 1965 or if a sticker indicates 0.004in or 0.10mm set both valves to 0.006in or 0.15mm
Cooling	Fan, driven directly from the crankshaft
Oil cooling	Horizontal oil-cooler in airstream from the fan
Static ignition timing	10° BTDC
Ignition advance	Centrifugal and vacuum August 1963 to July 1964; all others vacuum only
Firing order	1–4–3–2
Contact breaker gap	0.016in or 0.40mm
Carburettor	Twin Solex 32 PDSIT or 32 PDSIT-2 and 3, downdraught type

TYPE 4 1700CC TRANSPORTER

Type	4-stroke horizontally opposed air-cooled engine
Cylinders	4
Capacity	1679cc
Bore	90mm
Stroke	66mm
Compression ratio	7.8:1 carburettors, 8.2:1 fuel injection
Crankcase	Aluminium alloy
Cylinders	Individual cast iron, finned for air cooling
Cylinder head	Twin inlet-port cast aluminium, finned for air cooling
Crankshaft	Steel forging with four main bearings
Crankshaft end float	0.07 to 0.13mm
Main bearings 1, 3, 4	Circular sleeve bearings
Main bearing 2	Two bearing shells
Big-end bearings	Three-layer shells
Small-end bearings	Pressed-in bronze bushes
Pistons	Steel-reinforced aluminium alloy
Piston rings	Two compression and one oil control ring
Camshaft	Grey cast with three bearings running in aluminium shells
Camshaft drive	Helical gears from the crankshaft
Valves	Overhead
Valve clearances	0.006in or 0.015mm
Cooling	Fan, driven directly from the crankshaft
Oil cooling	Horizontal oil-cooler in airstream from the fan
Ignition timing	Single vacuum mostly 7.5° BTDC with hoses disconnected
	Double vacuum distributor 5° ATDC with hoses connected
	If in doubt, maximum advance at 2,500rpm should be no more than 32° BTDC. Conflicting data from various sources and dependent on the original distributor being fitted
Firing order	1–4–3–2
Contact breaker gap	0.016in or 0.40mm
Carburettor	Twin Solex 34 PDSIT-2 or 32 PDSIT-2, downdraught type

TYPE 4 1800CC TRANSPORTER

Type	4-stroke horizontally opposed air-cooled engine.
Cylinders	4
Capacity	1795cc
Bore	93mm
Stroke	66mm
Compression ratio	7.3:1 carburettors, 8.2:1 fuel injection
Crankcase	Aluminium alloy
Cylinders	Individual cast iron, finned for air cooling
Cylinder head	Twin inlet port cast aluminium, finned for air cooling
Crankshaft	Steel forging with four main bearings
Crankshaft end-float	0.07 to 0.13mm
Main bearings 1, 3, 4	Circular sleeve bearings
Main bearing 2	Two bearing shells
Big-end bearings	Three-layer shells
Small-end bearings	Pressed-in bronze bushes
Pistons	Steel-reinforced aluminium alloy
Piston rings	Two compression and one oil control ring
Camshaft	Grey cast with three bearings running in aluminium shells
Camshaft drive	Helical gears from the crankshaft
Valves	Overhead
Valve clearances	0.006in or 0.015mm
Cooling	Fan, driven directly from the crankshaft
Oil cooling	Horizontal oil-cooler in airstream from the fan
Ignition timing	Single vacuum mostly 7.5° BTDC with hoses disconnected
	Double vacuum distributor 5° ATDC with hoses connected
	With conflicting data from various sources and the correct settings dependent on the original distributor being fitted, this can be a minefield, so if in doubt, maximum advance at 2,500rpm should be no more than 32° BTDC
Firing order	1-4-3-2
Contact breaker gap	0.016in or 0.40mm
Carburettor	Twin Solex 34 PDSIT-2 or 32 PDSIT-2, downdraught type

TYPE 4 2000CC TRANSPORTER

Type	4-stroke horizontally opposed air-cooled engine
Cylinders	4
Capacity	1970cc
Bore	94mm
Stroke	71mm
Compression ratio	7.4:1 carburettors
Crankcase	Aluminium alloy
Cylinders	Individual cast iron, finned for air cooling
Cylinder head	Twin inlet-port cast aluminium, finned for air cooling
Crankshaft	Steel forging with four main bearings
Crankshaft end-float	0.07 to 0.13mm
Main bearings 1, 3, 4	Circular sleeve bearings
Main Bearing 2	Two bearing shells
Big-end bearings	Three-layer shells
Small-end bearings	Pressed-in bronze bushes
Pistons	Steel-reinforced aluminium alloy
Piston rings	Two compression and one oil control ring
Camshaft	Grey cast with three bearings running in aluminium shells
Camshaft drive	Helical gears from the crankshaft
Valves	Overhead
Valve clearances	0.006in or 0.015mm
Cooling	Fan, driven directly from the crankshaft
Oil cooling	Horizontal oil-cooler in airstream from the fan
Ignition timing	7.5° BTDC
	With conflicting data from various sources and the correct settings dependent on the original distributor being fitted, this can be a minefield, so if in doubt, maximum advance at 2,500rpm should be no more than 32° BTDC
Firing order	1–4–3–2
Contact breaker gap	0.016in or 0.40mm
Carburettor	Twin Solex 34 PDSIT, downdraught type
Fuel pump	Mechanical
Fuel injection	(if fitted) Bosch L-Jetronic with electric fuel pump

APPENDIX II

ENGINE AND CHASSIS NUMBERS

Fig App.1   The engine number on the Type 1 is below the generator stamped into the crankcase.

Fig App.2   The Beetle chassis number is located on the centre of the frame under the rear seat and is repeated on the vehicle identification plate under the front bonnet.

Fig App.3   The Bay Window Type 2 chassis number is situated to the left of the engine compartment. This is repeated on the vehicle identification plate.

Fig App.4   The engine number on 1700, 1800 and 2-litre engines is to the rear of the engine crankcase breather box.

RIGHT: *Fig App.5   The engine number on 1700, 1800 and 2-litre engines is repeated on the fan housing to the right of the coil.*

USEFUL ADDRESSES

PARTS SUPPLIERS

United Kingdom

VW Heritage
47 Dolphin Road
Shoreham-by-Sea, West Sussex
BN43 6PB

www.vwheritage.com
Phone: 01273 444000
Email: esales@vwheritage.com

Cool Air (GB) Ltd
Unit 4, Bilton Road, Erith, Kent
DA8 2AN

www.coolairvw.co.uk
Phone: 01322 33 50 50

Just Kampers
1 Stapeley Manor
Long Lane
Odiham, Hants
RG29 1JE

www.justkampers.com
Phone: 0800 9156 618

German and Swedish
Branches nationwide, including four outlets in Scotland, two in Wales and three in Ireland. Air-cooled parts are now sold under the name Vee Wee

www.gsfcarparts.com
Phone: 0121 626 7981

Mega-Bug
Unit 3
White Hart Road, London
SE18 1DG

www.megabug.co.uk
Phone: 0208 317 7333
Email: info@megabug.co.uk

C & C Custom and Commercial
Unit 11
Bookham Industrial Estate
Church Road, Great Bookham
Leatherhead, Surrey
KT23 3EU

www.customandcommercial.com
Phone: 01372 452 622
Email: info@customandcommercial.com

Justaircooled
43 Hermitage Road
Bridlington, East Yorkshire
YO16 4HF

Phone: 01262 671962 or 0800 888 6287

Kingfisher Kustoms
Unit 5
Oldbury Road, Smethwick
West Midlands
B66 1NU

Phone: 0121 558 9135
Email: sales@kkvw.co.uk

USEFUL ADDRESSES

Machine 7
Unit 2
Liberty Way
Attleborough Fields Industrial Estate
Nuneaton
Warwickshire
CV11 6RZ

Email: sales@machine7.com

Australia
VW Heritage
https://au.vwheritage.com

Classic Vee Dub
www.classicveedub.com.au
Phone: 03 9638 4200

DAS Resto Haus
6/2 Calabro Way,
Burleigh Heads
QLD 4220

https://dasrestohaus.com.au
Phone: 0417 645 854

Just Kampers Australia
PO Box 6287
Silverwater
NSW 1811

www.justkampers.com.au
Phone: 612 9645 7660

Australian Performance Centre
29 Research Drive
Croydon South
VIC 3136

avwpc@vwperformance.com.au
Phone: 03 9761 4540 or 03 9761 7917.
Fax: 03 9761 6216

Vollks Vee-Dub online store
www.vollks.com.au

Vintage Vee-Dub Supplies
Unit 1
118 Harp Street
Campsie
NSW 2194

Phone: 02 9789 1777
Fax: 02 9718 8704
Email: info@vintageveedub.com.au

Mick Motors
96 Old Toombul Road
Northgate
QLD 4013

Phone: 07 3266 8133
Fax: 07 3260 5179
Email: mick@mickmotors.com.au

USA
Wolfsburg West
2850 Palisades Drive
Corona
CA 92880

www.wolfsburgwest.com
Phone: 888 965 3937
Email: info@wolfsburgwest.com

J Bugs
1338 Rock Point Drive
Oceanside
CA 92056

www.jbugs.com
Phone: 800 231 1784
Email: sales@jbugs.com

California Import Parts Ltd
1124 Fir Avenue
PMB #108
Blaine Washington 98230

Phone: 604 946 0398 or 800 313 3811
Fax: 877 811 5111

USEFUL ADDRESSES

IPC Volkswagen Parts
14222 Prairie Avenue
Hawthorne
CA 90250

www.ipconlinestore.com
Phone: 310 644 7142

West Coast Metric Inc
24002 Frampton Avenue
Harbour City
CA 90710

www.westcoastmetric.com
Phone: 310 325 0005 or 800-247-3202
Email: info@westcoastmetric.com

Canada
California Import Parts Ltd
Unit 115
6780 Dennett Place
Delta, BC
V4G 1N4

WORKSHOP FACILITIES AND PARTS

Stateside Tuning
www.statesidetuning.co.uk
Phone: 01608 812438

The Engine Shop
Unit A2
Darenth Works, Ray Lamb Way
Erith, Kent
DA8 2SP

www.theengineshop.info
Phone: 01322 35022

Hulins Ltd (Gloucester).
Unit 1B
279 Bristol Road, Gloucester
GL2 5DD

Phone: 01452 50233

Beetlelink
Unit 2
Preymead Farm
Badshot Lea
Farnham
GU9 9LR

www.beetlelink.co.uk
Phone: 01252 326767
Email: info@beetlelink.co.uk

Jacks Garage (Transporter specialist)
20–22 Kingsdown Close
London
W10 6SW

www.jacksgarage.co.uk
Phone: 0207 243 8926
Email: Jacksgarage10@gmail.com

Dubtricks
Low Hall Farm
Dacre
Harrogate
HG3 4AA

www.dubtricks.co.uk
Phone: 01423 780147
Email: dubtricks@hotmail.co.uk

181 Classic Motors
Unit A6
Enterprise Business Park
Brunel Drive
Newark
Nottinghamshire
NG24 2DZ

www.181classicmotors.co.uk
Phone: 01636 918080 or 07725 05 29 96

GLOSSARY

Big-End Bearing The bearings in the connecting rod in contact with the crankshaft.

Camshaft A shaft with raised lobes that lift the valves in the combustion chamber.

Camshaft Drive Gear Helical gear mounted on the crankshaft to drive the camshaft.

Camshaft Plug A plug at the flywheel end of the crankcase, mounted in line with the camshaft. The rim of the plug is coated with Permatex during crankcase rebuild.

Clutch Driven Plate The plate holding the friction material that engages the drive when the pedal is released.

Clutch Pressure Plate The clutch component bolted to the flywheel that disengages the drive when the clutch pedal is pressed down.

Clutch Thrust Bearing When the clutch pedal is depressed the thrust bearing pushes the centre of the pressure plate to disengage the drive.

Connecting Rod Connects the piston to the crankshaft.

Crankshaft The main shaft of the engine.

Crankshaft Pulley Pulley mounted using a bolt directly to the rear of the crankshaft (on the Type 1 unit) to drive the generator and cooling fan via a drive belt.

Crankshaft Shims Three shims that are produced in various thicknesses to give a precise amount of free play between the flywheel and No. 1 main bearing.

Distributor Drive Gear Gear mounted on the crankshaft to drive the distributor drive shaft.

Distributor Drive Shaft Vertical shaft driven by a gear on the crankshaft to drive the distributor.

Fan (Type 1 Engine) The fan on the Type 1 engine is mounted on the front of the generator

Fan (Type 4 Engine) The fan is bolted to the fan hub.

Fan (Type 3 Engine) The fan along with the generator pulley is mounted, using a bolt directly to the rear of the crankshaft.

Fan Hub A hub mounted on the rear of the Type 4 unit to hold the fan.

Flywheel Dowels Short cylindrical bars that are a precise fit in both the crankshaft and flywheel. They are used to locate the flywheel to the crankshaft so that they stay locked together when the bolt is tightened. Engines that are highly tuned to give more power often use eight dowels instead of the usual four.

Gasket Usually thin paper or similar material used between metal surfaces of components to prevent leakage of oil or other liquids.

GLOSSARY

Gasket Sealant A jointing compound such as 'Permatex Super 300 Form-a –gasket sealant', used between the mating surfaces of the crankcase and on the camshaft plug.

Journal The bearing surfaces on the crankshaft and camshaft.

Main Bearing The bearings that support the crankshaft in the engine case.

Oil Strainer A wire gauze mesh encircling the oil pick-up tube within the engine. This is accessible for cleaning from under the engine unit during an oil-change service.

Oil Thrower Disc A concave disc, mounted concave side out to throw the oil back into the crankcase. This is in lieu of an oil seal at the pulley end. Not applicable to the Type 4 unit as this is fitted with an oil seal.

Piston Pin Also known as Gudgeon Pin. Connects the piston to the connecting rod.

Piston Pin Circlip Wire clips fitted in a groove in the piston each side of the piston pin to prevent lateral movement of the pin.

Piston Rings The VW units use three rings on the piston. The top one is the compression ring and the lowest is the oil scraper ring.

Push Rods Part of the valve train. Connects the valve lifter to the rocker.

Rocker Shaft Situated on the top of the cylinder head and holds the valve rockers.

Small-End Bearing The bearing in the connecting rod supporting the piston.

Split Valve Collets When fitted to the grooves on the valve shaft they form a cone that holds all the components of the valve assembly in place.

Suitcase-Style Engine A term to describe the units used in Type 3, Type 4 and the CT 1600cc engine fitted to some air-cooled T3 Transporter models. The fan is driven directly from the crankshaft, allowing a flatter design of fan housing to be used.

Tinware A general term to describe the metalwork around the engine. Most is used to direct the flow of air around the cylinders. It is also there to prevent hot air from the exhaust system from entering the engine bay and the cooling fan intake.

Torque Wrench Settings These are expressed in foot/pounds, shown as lb ft or Newton metres, shown as Nm.

Valve In this context they are situated in the cylinder head and allow the fuel mixture to flow in and the exhaust gas to be expelled.

Valve Adjustment Screw Also sometimes referred to as tappet screws. Fitted into each rocker and held in place by a lock nut, they allow the clearance between the screw and the valve stem to be adjusted.

Valve Keeper Holds the valve spring onto the valve stem and is held in place by the split collets.

Valve Lifters Also known as Tappets or Cam Followers – run against the lobes on the camshaft to lift the valves.

Valve Rocker One for each valve. Lifts the valve open via the tappet and the push rod.

Valve Spring Fitted to each valve, they compress to allow fuel and exhaust to pass in and out of the cylinder head.

Woodruff Key A 'D' shaped key that fits into a keyway on a shaft to locate gears and pulleys.

INDEX

accelerator cable   36, 113
air control flaps, 1700, 1800, 2-litre   115
air deflector plate, Type 1 cylinders   99
air filter vacuum pipes   38
air filter warm air elbow, Type 1
air filter warm air pipe, 1700, 1800, 2-litre   92, 115–117
air filter   17–21, 34
alternator and belt, 1700, 1800, 2-litre   93, 117–118

battery connection   30, 41
big-end bearings   65, 68, 71, 76

cam followers (*see also* tappets)   61–62, 69, 79
camshaft bearings   63, 79, 80
camshaft drive gear   73
camshaft end plug   63, 80
camshaft   63, 68, 80
carburettor hot spot tube   33
carburettor linkage   36
carburettor   46, 113–114
choke cable   36, 114
clutch pedal free play   25–26, 86–87
clutch   48, 85–87, 113
coil   42
condenser   23
connecting rods   61–62, 65, 76, 77
contact breaker points   23
crankcase sealant   62, 81
crankcase stud seals   63, 80
crankcase   61–62, 68, 78–90
crankshaft end float   64, 71, 80
crankshaft gears (see also distributor and camshaft gears)   66, 73

crankshaft oil deflector disc   15, 64–65
crankshaft oil seal (flywheel oil seal)   63, 68, 82
crankshaft oil seal, 1700, 1800, 2-litre rear   89
crankshaft pulley   51
crankshaft   68, 71, 80
cylinder barrels   60, 69, 98
cylinder cover (shrouds) tinware, Type 1   104
cylinder cover tinware, 1700, 1800, 2-litre   94–95, 121
cylinder head, 1700, 1800, 2-litre   90
cylinder head spacer shim   70
cylinder head studs   68
cylinder head tightening diagram   102
cylinder head   56, 59, 66, 69, 100–103

distributor, 1700, 1800, 2-litre   96, 119
distributor drive gear   66
distributor drive shaft   48, 55, 87–88
distributor   42, 48, 88

electrical connections   34
electrical connections, Type 4   39
engine installation   113–114
engine mountings, 1700, 1800, 2-litre   97, 122
engine mountings   36–37, 122
engine mountings, Transporter   38, 122
engine oil change   15–17
exhaust, 1700, 1800, 2-litre   96, 121–122
exhaust, Type 1   47, 111–113

fan, 1700, 1800, 2-litre   93, 117–118

INDEX

fan belt, Type 1 engine   12, 42, 108
fan housing, 1700, 1800, 2-litre   92–93, 117
fan housing air deflector boxes   44
fan housing throttle ring, 25, 30, early 34PS only   43, 108–109
fan housing, Type 1 engine   33, 42, 107
fan hub, 1700, 1800 and 2-litre   54, 61, 89, 117–118
flywheel 1700, 1800 and 2-litre   54, 89
flywheel bolt(s)   53, 65, 89
flywheel dowels   71
flywheel oil seal (crankshaft oil seal)   63
flywheel, Type 1   11, 52–53, 61, 84
fuel pipe   32, 38, 41
fuel pump, Type 1 engine   22, 44, 110–111
fuel pump, 1700, 1800, 2-litre   91, 119

generator drive belt, Type 3   14
generator support, Type 1   106–107
generator, alternator   42, 107–108
gudgeon pins (piston pins)   76

heat exchanger, 1700, 1800 and 2-litre   90, 95, 120
heat exchanger, Type 1 engine   32, 47, 111
heater box   47–48
heater cable   32
heater fan, 1700, 1800, 2-litre   120
heater hoses, 1700, 1800, 2-litre   40–41, 120
heater hoses, Type 1 engine   31

ignition leads   25, 42, 45
ignition system   23–25
inlet manifold, Type 1 single port   104–105
inlet manifold, Type 1 twin-port   105

line-bored case   68

main bearing dowel   63, 66, 68, 78–79
main bearing shells   63–64, 71, 78
main bearing   68, 71–73, 80

oil breather, 1700, 1800, 2-litre   117
oil cooler, 1700, 1800, 2-litre   91, 115

oil cooler, Type 1 engine   48–49, 68, 104–106
oil cooler, Type 1 engine, dog leg type   44, 106, 109–110
oil deflector disc   64–65, 73
oil filler tube, 1700, 1800, 2-litre   40, 92, 119
oil filter, external spin-on type   29, 117
oil pressure relief valve and oil control valve   82
oil pressure warning light switch   91
oil pressure warning light switch, 1700, 1800, 2-litre   120, 122
oil pump   55, 62, 69, 82–84
oil pump, semi-automatic Type 1.   55
oil strainer   49, 84

piston rings   98–99
piston   60–61, 69, 98–99
push rod tubes   59–60, 69, 101–102
push rod tubes, 1700, 1800, 2-litre   89–90, 101
push rod   58–59, 102

raising the vehicle   30–31
rocker box cover   56–57
rocker shaft   57–59, 67, 103

semi-automatic auto-transmission fluid pipes   35
semi-automatic clutch solenoid   35
semi-automatic torque converter   35
semi-automatic Type 1 engine removal   35
small-end bearings   76
spark plug gap   25
spark plug   24, 56
static ignition timing   23–24
stud removal   56

thermostat cable, 1700, 1800, 2-litre   115–116
thermostat   32, 44, 109
throttle ring, 25, 30 and early 34PS only   43, 108–109
tinware   33, 44, 42, 48, 85, 111
transporter foam engine surround   38

transporter fuel tank   8
transporter rear valence   38
Type 1 twin-port cylinder head   44, 46
Type 1 twin-port inlet manifold   45–46
Type 3 carburettor linkage   39
Type 3 fan housing bellows   39
Type 3 torque converter   39
Type 4, 411 and 412 gearbox input shaft   41

valve clearences (tappet adjustment)   27–29, 70, 103
valve guide   67, 70, 73
valve removal   66
valve spring   101
valves   70, 100–101

Woodruff key   64, 72–73, 85

RELATED TITLES FROM CROWOOD

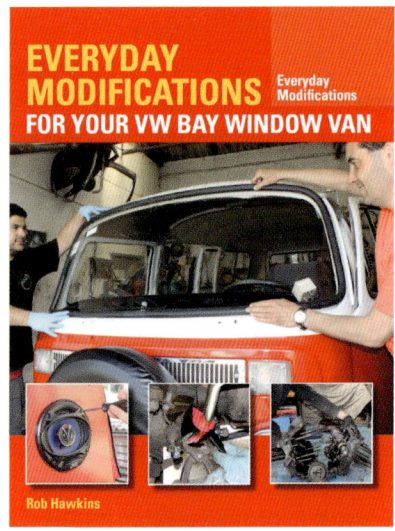

Everyday Modifications for Your VW Bay Window Van
ROB HAWKINS
ISBN 978 1 84797 913 1
192pp, 730 illustrations

VW Beetle Specification Guide 1949–1967
JAMES RICHARDSON
ISBN 978 1 86126 940 9
128pp, 300 illustrations

VW Transporter and Microbus Specification Guide 1950–1967
DAVID ECCLES
ISBN 978 1 86126 652 1
96pp, 400 illustrations

VW Transporter and Microbus Specification Guide 1967–1979
VINCENT MOLENAAR AND ALEXANDER PRINZ
ISBN 978 1 84797 480 8
128pp, 470 illustrations

In case of difficulty ordering, please contact the Sales Office:

The Crowood Press, Ramsbury, Wiltshire SN8 2HR UK

Tel: 44 (0) 1672 520320   enquiries@crowood.com   www.crowood.com